Writing Handbooks

Writing Sitcoms

John Byrne &
Marcus Powell

D1079845

A & C Black • London

First published 2003
A & C Black Publishers Limited
37 Soho Square, London W1D 3QZ
www.acblack.com

© 2003 John Byrne and Marcus Powell

ISBN 0–7136–6526–2

A CIP catalogue record for this book is
available from the British Library.

The episode from *Do Nothing 'Til You Hear From Me*
(pp. 58–90) is reproduced by permission of the BBC;
the extracts from *Stage Fright* (pp. 97–114) are
reproduced by permission of Nicci Crowther and
Squeeze Productions.

A & C Black uses paper produced with elemental
chlorine-free pulp, harvested from managed
sustainable forests.

Typeset in 10½ on 12½pt Sabon
Printed and bound in Great Britain by
Creative Print and Design (Wales), Ebbw Vale

Contents

Acknowledgements

M.P. Without the inspiration of other writers and performers, this book would never have been undertaken, and as such I would like to thank the following: John Byrne, for opening up a whole other area of creativity for me; Geoffrey Aymer, with whom I shared those first steps as a comedy writer; Martin Glynn for his generosity of spirit and practical advice towards a relatively inexperienced writer; Yvette Rochester-Duncan for being a fine actress and bringing my work to life on so many occasions, and as such, inspiring me to write more; Sam Kelly for not only being a first-rate actor, but also a very nice man, helping to create the most enjoyable night of my professional life; my past collaborators, Andrew Murrell and Junior Simpson for their exchange of ideas, tolerance of my 11th hour changes, and their respective comedic abilities, and lastly, but *definitely* most importantly, my family: my little boy Khaya, a budding writer and Daddy's little genius, and my wife Lunga, without whom none of this would matter anyway.

J.B. John would like to thank God, his wife and family and Marcus, without all of whom his real-life sitcom would be a lot less amusing.

Introduction

Since you are taking the time to at least look at this book, it's safe to assume that you have a passing interest in the craft of writing sitcoms. Perhaps our subtitle should be '*It's Up To You!*', since what we can't do is write a sitcom for you!

We love sitcoms! Let's qualify that immediately – we love *good* sitcoms! This may seem a fairly obvious statement, as it's unlikely that anyone would relish the prospect of sitting through endless episodes of a spectacularly bad one (unless they had some sort of masochistic streak) or would spend time writing about a subject they absolutely loathed (unless they were doing it as some form of therapy). As to what actually constitutes a *good* sitcom, this is, of course, open to interpretation, although 'the ability to make the audience laugh until soup comes out of their noses' is a pretty good yardstick!

While we can't promise that after reading this you'll produce the next *Steptoe and Son* or *Frasier,* or become the new John Sullivan or Galton and Simpson (and if your response to those names is 'Who?' then you need this book more than we realised), what we do intend to try and do is give you a clearer understanding of the methods used and rules adhered to by sitcom writers since the genre was invented on radio, as far back as 1926. By applying these rules and methods to your own work, you stand a greater chance of achieving success. What you write about, however, is . . . (refer to subtitle).

In the course of this book, we'll be looking at characters, settings and plots, as well as some of the areas to consider once you've actually completed your script, such as selling your ideas, recording etc. We'll be using examples from various sitcoms as well as hypothetical situations to illustrate our points throughout the chapters. To that end, we have also included scenes from some of our own scripted efforts over the years. We

1

hope you find them instructive . . . (and 'funny' would be nice as well).

As well as the rules and methods mentioned, we have also taken a look at some of the major contributors to the genre over the past 50 years. Many of the programmes mentioned are readily available on video, DVD, audio tape, cable TV etc, not to mention published scripts in that old-fashioned device for gaining information – books! Our resource section at the back will give you some idea of what's available.

Who knows, if all you gain from reading this book is a desire to discover the delights of *The Navy Lark* or *Shelley*, then our time here will not have been wasted. However, it would be even more rewarding if you were inspired to create your own sitcom which went on to provide as much enjoyment as those great series.

We hope you enjoy reading this as much as we have enjoyed writing it, and if we've enjoyed writing it half as much as you enjoy reading it, then you'll enjoy reading it twice as much as us . . . or something!

Marcus Powell & John Byrne 2003

1. The sitcom

We all have our favourite sitcoms. What's yours? *'Fawlty Towers! Dad's Army! Cheers! Only Fools and Horses!'* you cry. *'It was a rhetorical question!'* we scream.

Some viewers may cite *Frasier* as the funniest 30 minutes of sophisticated comedic shenanigans, wedged either side of a commercial break, it has ever been their good fortune to witness. Others may have a fond hankering for the 'Room for one on top?' 'Not 'alf!' nudge-nudge naughtiness of an *On The Buses*. Whatever your preference or preferences, it's likely that at some time or other (faced with an assault on the senses in the name of humour, coming directly from the rectangular one-eyed babysitter in the corner of your very own living room) we have all thought to ourselves: 'I could come up with something better than this!'

Of course, very few of us actually try and put this claim into practice, but for those who do, the road ahead is bumpy, and not for the faint hearted, with obstacles aplenty and miles of rewrites before you sleep . . . Oh, alright, so perhaps writing a sitcom isn't exactly like becoming Master Frodo of the Shire setting out to return the ring, and the most fearsome sight you'll ever encounter is probably only that of a script editor suffering from sleep deprivation, wielding nothing more dangerous than a red pen. However, for all the good humour and satisfaction that a finished sitcom can produce, the journey to the end credits is a serious business. A business that can make even writers who are supremely gifted in other areas of comedy, hesitate before leaping into it. Victoria Wood, an undoubted expert in the field of both comedic writing and performing, is cited as having wanted to write a sitcom as far back as 1979. The fact that she didn't feel ready to produce *dinnerladies* until 1998, says as much about the difficulty of the task, as her own exacting standards.

3

Okay, assuming you haven't already ditched this book in favour of the new Terry Pratchett, let's help you take those first steps towards writing your own sitcom. Just think of us as your personal Grey Wizards. (Alright, alright! We promise . . . No more of the Tolkien allusions! Cos if you haven't read the books or seen the films, you're gonna think we're just . . . weird!)

The analytical eye

Permit us a quote. We'd love to be able to take credit for it, but that must go to Ma-Chu, Master of the art of Haiku. It holds as true for writers of sitcoms as it does for three-line Japanese poetry:

> First you have to learn the form – next you have to master the form.

> When you have accomplished both of these important things, then, and then alone, you have the freedom to create.

Eastern philosophy always sounds very deep, so let's put it another way: *Know your onions!*

First things first. Once you have made a decision to write a sitcom, you have to start looking at them differently. No, not with one eye shut, peering out from behind the sofa, or doing the crossword while de-fleaing the dog, but *analytically*. Choose one of your aforementioned 'favourites', videotape them, then sit down with a notepad and pencil and really watch them. Try to figure out why they work as well as they do. For the moment, we'll take it as read that they're funny – the question you have to figure out is: Why?

Conversely, have a proper look at a sitcom you absolutely loathe. Study each scene, trying to remain objective (between the tears and gnashing of teeth), and assess why the dialogue doesn't work. Sometimes 'It's not funny' may just sum it up – but try to dig a little deeper. How would you improve it? Why aren't the characters believable/likeable? How would you change them? Did the plot twists confuse you/bore you/annoy you? What would you do to resolve them? If you could dictate the outcome of the plot five minutes into the show, how would you have made it more unpredictable? Fair enough, you may not have answers to these questions immediately, but once you start raising the questions, you're beginning to think like a sitcom writer. You'll probably still wind up hating the said show, but at least now, instead of just having an adverse reaction to it, you'll be able to say exactly why you dislike it. And, by studying it closely, you will, hopefully, have a better understanding of what not to do when it comes to writing your own.

Make a note of each scene. It may have lasted only a minute, but in that minute, what were the writers doing? Did the dialogue move the plot along, or was it just an excuse for one of the characters to say something funny? Well, if the writers have done their job, the scene did both. Did the writers drop in a reference early in the episode, which at the time just seemed like a passing gag but later on proved to be more significant? For example, in one of our scripted efforts, this time for radio, we had a character throwing a stone up against a window, trying to attract the attention of the person within, accidentally breaking the glass. The plot moved on, only for the pay-off of the episode to see the vindictive homeowner have our innocent character arrested for attempted burglary.

Look at the way the characters change over the course of the episode. In a recent episode of *Friends*, Monica decides to pay Chandler a visit while he is working away from home. Turning up at his hotel unexpectedly, she surprises him as he is enjoying the dubious delights of pay-per-view porn. Sensing what he is up to, she is further shocked to discover that he is actually becoming aroused watching a programme about shark attacks . . . or so she thinks. Not realising that Chandler had switched channels at the last minute, Monica is convinced that her husband is a freak with a Jaws fetish (giving a whole new meaning to the term 'Deep Blue Sea'). However, instead of filing for divorce, Monica decides to try and indulge her husband in his fantasy, to the point of renting shark video tapes to try and get him in the mood, but not before spending the duration of the episode enquiring amongst the female Friends as to whether or not Chandler's condition is common . . . or just her luck! Of course the whole thing is resolved, when a highly confused Chandler confesses to having been watching regular old porn, much to Monica's relief and Chandler's amazement and deeper understanding of his wife's love for him. Unlikely, perhaps, but certainly a development in both their characters . . . and very funny it was too.

Of course, the Monica/Chandler situation was just one strand of this episode of *Friends*. Joey was doubtless doing something horny or stupid, or both. Phoebe was being kooky all over the place, Rachel was her usual sexy and neurotic self, and Ross was having the same old trouble . . . finishing . . . his . . . *sentences*. In short, a fine example of an ensemble show, with clearly defined and well-loved characters.

The style of the show is something else to think about while watching your videotapes and making your notes. Classic comedies like *M*A*S*H*, *Drop The Dead Donkey*, *Are You Being Served?*, *It Ain't Half Hot Mum*, *Taxi!*, *Soap*, *The Golden Girls*, are all further examples of series without an individual character at the helm. True, we all have our favourite characters from these shows. It's probably fair to say that Alan Alda's Hawkeye Pierce had the lion's share of the laughs amongst the members of the 4077th, and you may have had a penchant for Mrs Slocombe's feline activities, over, say, John Inman's regular offer of something for nothing, but none of these characters were definitively 'central'. However, in *The Phil Silvers Show*, for example, if 'Bilko' wasn't doing something, the show wasn't doing *anything*! Very definitely a star vehicle for Mr Silvers then, which isn't to say that the supporting cast were mere cardboard cutouts. Colonel Hall's bluff and bluster was a vital ingredient to the show, and where would an ace wheeler-dealer like Bilko be without suckers like Sgt. Ritzik to rip off? No, it's just that the writers (a young Neil Simon amongst them) decided to place the comedy ball very firmly in Phil's court, and very successfully too, for while other sitcoms of a similar vintage have long since faded into memory, Bilko is still being shown almost 50 years after it first aired.

Star vehicle sitcoms were very much the fashion during the golden age of TV, with shows built around the comedic personalities of the likes of George Burns & Gracie Allen, Jackie Gleason in *The Honeymooners*, and of course, Lucille Ball in her various series. It's interesting to note that the performers chose situation comedy as a vehicle for their respective talents, rather than the seemingly more straightforward sketch or variety formats. Even Bing Crosby strolled his way through 28 episodes of his own domestic sitcom in the mid 60s.

In the UK, the likes of Arthur Askey, Eric Sykes and Jimmy Edwards all dabbled in the comedy of situation. Jimmy Edwards (via Messrs Frank Muir and Denis Norden) starred in a series of seven self-contained half hours called *The Faces of Jim*, each allowing him to play a different character within the context of the story each week. Although this was probably just an excuse for the much-moustachioed Jim to dress up and indulge in different voices, providing the audience with a great laugh each week, the idea of a series of self-contained narratives proved very useful when Galton and Simpson created their *BBC Playhouse* series of one-offs, which was to spawn the mighty *Steptoe and Son*. Ronnie Barker also had his own *Playhouse* series of self-contained half hours in the late 60s. Unquestionably, the most popular sitcom star of the 1950s and 60s was 'the lad himself' Tony Hancock, who after three years of cracking them up on radio, moved into people's living rooms via the small screen and proceeded to crack them up all over again. Actually, *Hancock's Half Hour* ran simultaneously on radio and TV until 1960, with Ray Galton and Alan Simpson providing two completely different sets of scripts for the two mediums.

Genres

The majority of these shows were in the vein of domestic comedy: Father/Mother dealing with crazy antics of spouse and/or children (*Bless This House, Father, Dear Father, Keep It In The Family, Butterflies, No Place Like Home, The Cosby Show* etc, right up to more recent offerings like *My Family* and *Barbara*). The chalk and cheese/flatshare set-up is another sitcom staple: the posh one and the working class one, the messy one and the tidy one etc – *The Likely Lads, The Liver Birds, Two In Clover* (with Sid James and Victor Spinetti), *The Odd Couple*, the aforementioned *Steptoe and Son*, and, for many series, Sid James and Tony Hancock. More contemporary series such as *Will & Grace, Absolutely Fabulous* and *Men Behaving Badly* could loosely fit into this category, although it's probably more correct to call these 'chalk and chalk' comedies, as Ab Fab's Edina and Patsy, and 'Men's' Gary and Tony seem to be cut very much from the same rabble rousing cloth.

Another example of the 'chalk and cheese' type show is the 'fish out of water' scenario: *Mork and Mindy, The Fresh Prince of Bel-Air, Perfect Strangers* (following the exploits of a

Mediterranean shepherd who travels to Chicago to live with his American cousin). There are, of course, just as many series set in the workplace, for example: *The Rag Trade, On The Buses* and the short lived *Odd Man Out* (which featured John Inman as the owner of a Littlehampton rock factory). In more recent times, the trend has been towards shows about 20/30-somethings coming to terms with adulthood and relationships etc: *Friends, Coupling, Cold Feet, Sex and the City, Two Pints of Lager and a Packet of Crisps* – to name but a few.

Radio

We'll be looking at characters and settings in more detail in subsequent chapters. For the moment, let's refer back to your 'favourite' show on videotape. What category does it fall into? Perhaps it is none of the above. Perhaps it isn't even on TV at all. Radio is, of course, the other prime medium for the sitcom writer. Like *Hancock's Half Hour*, many successful TV sitcoms had their beginnings on radio: *Second Thoughts, After Henry, An Actor's Life For Me, The Hitch-Hiker's Guide to the Galaxy, The Secret Diary of Adrian Mole, aged 13¾* etc, the last two titles, of course, making their way via adaptations of hugely successful novels. Conversely, there are many TV series that have later been specially adapted and re-recorded for radio, amongst them, *Dad's Army, Shelley, To The Manor Born* and *Yes, Minister*.

Radio itself spawned many sitcoms which never appeared on the small screen, and yet played to consistently large and loyal audiences for many years, such as *The Navy Lark* (which ran for 13 series over 18 years, and featured such fine comic actors as Jon Pertwee, Leslie Philips and Ronnie Barker), and *The Men From The Ministry* (which ran for 15 years). There were, however, just as many radio sitcoms which, despite a fine pedigree in both the writing and performing department, failed for one reason or another to stand the test of time. For example, *Finkel's Café* by Frank Muir and Denis Norden and starring none other than Peter Sellers and Sidney James (a comedic dream team by anybody's reckoning), ran for only nine episodes during 1956 before all concerned went on to fry larger fish.

In some ways it is easy to look upon radio as something of a poor relation to TV. To think that way, however, is to do the medium a criminal disservice. It isn't simply 'telly without the pictures!' Writing a script for radio is, in our experience, one of the most creatively freeing experiences a writer can have when dealing with material for performance. In many ways the only restriction is one of your own imagination. Naturally, however, there are certain rules to be adhered to when writing for sound only. Let's give you a for instance:

On screen, two characters (let's call them Tom and Joan) can be having a conversation about the morning paper failing to arrive, yet again. A third character (let's call her Daphne) can make her presence felt, simply by silently entering the room, crossing to the window . . . and pulling out a revolver. Now, perhaps Daphne's entrance went unnoticed by Tom and Joan . . . But, the audience would still witness the entrance, the gun etc, and, if after firing a couple of rounds Daphne exited, leaving Joan to pass a remark about her curiosity as to the newsagents sending out four different paperboys in as many days, the 'joke' would still register.

Now, how would that same, simple scene work in a radio sitcom? Well, for a start, Daphne's entrance could not go 'unnoticed' by Tom and Joan; otherwise, it would also have to go unnoticed by the audience. Short of Daphne entering, mumbling to herself something along the lines of 'Now where did I leave that bullet . . . ?' (which might tip off the joke, somewhat), without a 'Hi Daph' from one of the other characters, the listener would never know she was there at all.

Now, suppose through some terribly witty (but brief) exposition, you did establish Daphne's presence in the room prior to her firing of the gun, there are several stages you have to go through before the punchline. Well, for a start, she wasn't in the room when the scene began, so you would have to indicate via sound effects that the door has been opened. To add to that, you could also have Daphne's footsteps walking across the floor. Thirdly, you could have the sound of the window opening. Once the window has been opened, you could have the sound of birds chirping outside. This would, of course, indicate early morning, and if this sound was coupled with the equally chirpy approaching whistle of the delivery boy, and possibly the sound of a bicycle, we would immediately establish that the youth is in close proximity to the house. Follow this up with the sound of a revolver being cocked, a bang, and a distant yelp, then add the sounds of the window being closed, Daphne's footsteps walking away, and the door gently closing, and you have all the makings of an assassination attempt . . . in sound. Now, if in your script you have written that in the background of all these sound effects Tom and Joan have been chatting away amongst themselves, you give the suggestion that they have paid no attention to Daphne, or the shooting, making Joan's last line about the unexplained turnover of paperboys all the more amusing . . . Potentially.

If all of this seems like a lot of bother to go to just for what is, at best, a very silly gag, then perhaps writing for radio isn't for you. As we stated before, the beauty of radio is the opportunity to stretch the imagination of both writer and audience – which isn't to in any way suggest that you can't do that with the visual medium, just that in radio the thought processes are slightly different. If, for example, one of your characters dreams that they are being swept off their feet by Clark Gable (a show aimed at the youth market, obviously), and your radio script demands a re-enactment of *Gone With The Wind*, complete with 'the burning of Tara', with the right sound effects and actors, it can be done. Now, try getting that idea past even the most enthusiastic TV producer, and, despite your most articulate protestations as to why the scene should stay in, you'll find that 'frankly my dear, they don't give a . . . ' Well, you get the idea! While a series on radio can't compete with TV when it comes to profile, a series on radio also doesn't have to compete with TV when it comes to budgets. A quartet of good character actors can sound like a cast of 30, at no extra cost. A myriad exotic 'locations' are available at the flick of a sound cue. As you may have guessed, we are passionate advocates of radio and feel that, for writers with a love of dialogue especially, there is no greater medium.

If your only exposure to sitcoms has been through television, and you think that the gadget above the lighter on your dashboard is just there to pump out the Top 40, open yourself up to the delights of Radio 2 and 4. The BBC has a superb range of programmes on tape (some we've already mentioned, others you'll have the pleasure of discovering for yourself), and we highly recommend that you purchase some of them immediately. Well, not just now . . . but as soon as you finish reading this!

Animation

Another potential avenue for your work is the animated sitcom. It could be argued that the first series of this type was *The Flintstones*, which was based on the aforementioned *Honeymooners*, starring 50s US comedy star Jackie Gleason, while *Top Cat* was loosely derived from 'Bilko'. By the early 70s there was a proliferation of straight ahead animated versions of top series such as *The Addams Family*, *The Partridge Family*, (and just to show that single people also got a look in) *I Dream Of Jeannie*, *Happy Days*, *Mork and Mindy* etc. *Wait 'Til Your Father Gets Home* was an original domestic animated sitcom aimed at adults (the next-door neighbour looked like Richard Nixon!), as opposed to the kid-friendly offerings that went before, and could be viewed as a forerunner of *The Simpsons*. It took the anarchic satire of Bart and family to make TV audiences realize that cartoons weren't just for the little ones, and that animation could be used to put forward myriad comedic ideas beyond the comparatively simple (yet no less brilliant – no letters please!) escapades of Yogi Bear et al. Excellent adult animated fare has followed in the wake of *The Simpsons'* success, such as *King of the Hill*, *Family Guy*, *Futurama*, and of course, *South Park*, to name but a few. The UK threw their hat into the ring with, amongst others, *Pond Life* and *Stressed Eric*. In many ways (apart from the obvious) animated sitcoms are like radio, in that they allow the writer far more scope for characters and locations etc, without having to worry as much about budgetary restrictions in the same way as you would in a live action series.

To put our money where our reputations are, we've taken the liberty of including an example of an original script for an animated sitcom, entitled *Life–1, Bloke–Nil*.

Life–1, Bloke–Nil

(The adventures of an angst-ridden dollop)

An animated sitcom by Marcus Powell.

Pre-credit sequence:
The camera tracks across the London skyline at night, to the strains of a tinkling jazz piano. We close in on the second floor window of a three-storey terraced house. The camera pans across the living room, over the litter-strewn floor, past the well-used settee, and along the wall, passing a framed photograph of a rather smug looking cat. The camera finally rests on a closed door as the music fades. From behind the door we hear the voice of Darren, moaning ecstatically.

DARREN: . . . Ooh, I like that. Oh, yeh . . . That's good . . . That's really . . . Oh, yeh . . . Yeh . . . Oh, that's nice that is . . .

CHLOE: Darren . . . do I have to swallow? I mean, do you mind if I don't this time?

DARREN: Well, it would be very nice if you could do that little thing for me, Chloe . . . Yes, it . . . er . . . definitely would . . .

CHLOE: But, couldn't I just . . . sort of . . . 'sloosh' it around a bit?

DARREN: Well . . . Yeh, I suppose you could . . . if you like . . . but, if you love me, I'd really like you to take it all down.

CHLOE: Oh . . . alright . . . Gulp . . . *(Pause, then sounds of violent vomiting)*

DARREN: *(Pause)* . . . I'll get a cloth.

The door opens to reveal Darren, a thin, lugubrious looking man in his late twenties, fully dressed in a faded t-shirt, jeans and trainers. He wears Chris Evans style glasses, a cropped haircut, and a wispy goatee beard, but no moustache. He is holding a glass of beer. Behind him, sitting on the edge of the bed, also fully clothed, is Chloe, an extremely attractive, (if rather ill at the moment) stylishly dressed young woman. She is also holding a glass of beer, but as far away from her face as possible.

DARREN: *(To himself)* Honestly, you'd think most women would jump at the chance of a bit of 'Home Brew'.

CUT TO TITLES AND MUSIC

FADE TO–

Scene One:
Darren and Chloe are snuggled up on the settee, in front of a flickering television set. Chloe is fast asleep, while Darren is engrossed in the visions on the screen. From the sound of Celine Dion warbling, we can deduce that he is watching 'Titanic'. The cat, seen earlier in the photograph, jumps on to the arm of the settee, next to Darren.

DARREN: *(To cat)* Hello, Tibby. Hello, boy. *(He tickles the cat under his chin)* That's a good boy. Yes, that's a good boy. You like it when 'Daddy' does that, don't you . . . ?

DR PHIBES: *(George Sanders type voice)* Actually, may I just say, speaking as an animal who possesses the ability to lick my own genitalia, your systematic mauling of my larynx in this cack-handed display of affection, provides me with little or no thrill whatsoever. Oh, and while we're on the subject, it would please me beyond belief, if you would refrain from addressing me as 'Tibby', in future. It's a rather childish sobriquet, and one I don't much care for. Henceforth, you shall refer to me as 'Dr Phibes'.

DARREN: *(Pause, stunned)* Tibby . . . You can . . . Talk!!!

DR PHIBES: Ah, yes. In the time honoured tradition of animated animals being bestowed with human characteristics, it would appear that I have been endowed with a verbal dexterity far superior to that of my, ahem, 'owner'.

DARREN: . . . Yeh, but you can *talk*.

DR PHIBES: As well . . .

Chloe stirs, and then begins to snore gently.

DR PHIBES: I see that the ingénue in this badly drawn vignette is ensconced in the land of nod.

DARREN: Yeh. Poor Chloe. She just couldn't keep her eyes open, 'my little ookums'. It's a shame, cos she really wanted to see 'Titanic' again. Total 'chick flick', mind you, but not bad. (*He nuzzles her as she sleeps*)

DR PHIBES: Yes, I can fully appreciate how a film depicting the mass destruction of thousands of human beings, could provide an immeasurable source of amusement. Indeed that very subject matter is a constant topic of discussion amongst my colleagues and I. However, no matter how far we may progress in our campaign plans, we cannot escape the annoyingly irrefutable fact 'that tin openers require *fingers*.' Curses!

DARREN: (*Oblivious, to Chloe, lovingly, as he nuzzles her*) What are we gonna do with you, eh, little miss sleepyhead?

DR PHIBES: We could consider eating her . . .

DARREN: Pardon.

DR PHIBES: Nothing. Merely a regurgitated hair-ball. Ahem.

There is a sudden crash from the flat above, followed by gales of laughter from at least half a dozen people. Darren and Dr Phibes slowly raise their eyes to the ceiling.

DARREN: (*After a beat*) That bloke upstairs gets right on my tits!

DR PHIBES: How so?

DARREN: Well, he's always . . . doing something, isn't he . . . ?

DR PHIBES: Is he?

DARREN: Yeh, he's one of those . . . 'tossy' . . . popular blokes.

DR PHIBES: Indeed . . .

DARREN: *(Ranting)* Yeh, I mean, if he isn't having a dinner party with his 'up your bum' mates in 'publishing' or something, probably giving them an 'oh-so-amusing' account of the first time he ever went diving for oysters in the Seychelles with Sean Connery, and had to wrestle his virile chest hairs from the tentacles of a passing squid 'who turned out to be a George Lazenby fan, ho ho ho'; then, he's in training to run the marathon backwards dressed as a Pringle to raise money to rescue some rare albino polecat found nesting in a dormant volcano, and oh, guess what, 'Lah de bloody dah', *he's* the only one qualified to bungee jump down and rescue the obscure little verminous twat.

DR PHIBES: *(After a beat)* Am I to take it from that venomous outpouring, that basically you suspect Chloe finds him physically attractive . . . ?

DARREN: Like a bitch on heat!

Darren and Dr Phibes simultaneously gaze up at the ceiling as another muffled burst of laughter ensues.

FADE TO–

Scene Two:
Darren and Chloe are laying in bed naked.

DARREN: Chloe, would you say we had a good sex life?

CHLOE: Sorry, in what sense 'good' . . . ?

DARREN: Well, in the sense that you wouldn't rather smear marmalade into your crotch, and have your bikini line waxed by an army of worker ants.

CHLOE: Oh . . . *(Pause)* Then, 'yes'.

DARREN: Is that your *final* answer? You sure you don't want to 'phone a friend' . . . ?

CHLOE: Sorry, it's just that you took me a bit by surprise. I mean, it isn't normally something that seems to bother you.

DARREN:	(*Suddenly defensive*) I didn't say it *bothered* me. I just thought I'd get your *take* on it, that's all. I mean, you are *involved* as well.
CHLOE:	Well, actually, Darren, now that you mention it, I do sometimes feel like a bit of a footnote to your libido.
DARREN:	Are you saying that I just use you to gratify myself sexually?
CHLOE:	No, not always . . . Just whenever we're having sex.

CUT TO–

Scene Three:
Darren is in the bath. Dr Phibes sits on the edge of the bath, staring down and pawing at the water between Darren's legs.

DARREN:	. . . Could you stop doing that please . . . ?
DR PHIBES:	My apologies. So, what happened then?
DARREN:	Well, then she started spouting some pseudo 'Men are from Mars/Women are from Ikea' load of old arse, about love and where the relationship's heading and . . . and stuff (*Pause*) And there was I thinking we were talking about shagging . . .
DR PHIBES:	Perplexing.
DARREN:	So then I asked her straight out, 'are you knocking a piece off that bloke upstairs?' Well, she didn't see that coming, I can tell you . . .
DR PHIBES:	Yes, I can well see how that conversational shift would put her at somewhat of a disadvantage, considering the fact that, to my knowledge, she has never exchanged a word with your neighbour upstairs.
DARREN:	Yes, she said that too. (*Pause*) Then she left me.
DR PHIBES:	Interesting. (*Pause*) And what exactly were you hoping to achieve with that particular line of enquiry?

DARREN:	Well . . . I . . . I don't know. I mean, I'd just had sex, for God's sake . . .
DR PHIBES:	And were thereby incapable of rational thought . . . ?
DARREN:	Exactly.
DR PHIBES:	Well, have you considered the possible ramifications of your post-coital accusatory outbursts?

Close-up of Darren with his eyes whirling like a slot machine pay line, eventually reading 'Empty'.

DR PHIBES:	Perhaps I may be allowed to venture a supposition . . . ? You have taken a perfectly loyal and extremely tolerant woman, a woman who, hitherto, would no sooner think of being unfaithful than I would of appearing with Twiggy in an advert for the Canine Defence League, and planted a seed of infidelity in her mind.
DARREN:	I . . . I don't understand. (*Pause*) Actually, I think I've got a bit of soap stuck up my bum.
DR PHIBES:	(*To himself*) Ah, 'the perch is swinging, the bell is ringing, but the canary is long since dead.' Due to your insecurities, you may have forced Chloe, the only other person to have genuinely noticed the similarity between your scrotal birthmark and Thora Hird in profile, into the arms of your imagined rival.
DARREN:	(*Pause, then*) Nah, she wouldn't do that. I mean, I know she's a bit pissed off with me at present, but . . . Nah she wouldn't really cheat on me. (*Pause*) Not with him.

Suddenly we hear the sounds of a squeaking bed from the flat above.

DR PHIBES:	'Curiosity killed the cat.' (*He shudders*) A loathsome expression, but one that may prove to be quite apposite in this instance.

Darren and Dr Phibes look up simultaneously towards the sound. The camera pans up towards the ceiling. As Darren and Dr Phibes leave the frame, Dr Phibes' gaze returns to the water between Darren's legs.

DARREN: (*Off screen*) Oh bollocks!

We hear the sound of water gently lapping.

DARREN: (*Off screen*) I asked you to stop doing that.

DR PHIBES: (*Off screen*) My apologies.

CUT TO–

Scene Four:
Chloe stands by the front door, carrying several bags. She is very upset.

CHLOE: Okay . . . Well . . . I'll send someone for the rest of my things.

DARREN: Okay.

CHLOE: . . . Alright then.

DARREN: Alright then.

CHLOE: Is there nothing you want to say to me, Darren?

DARREN: Um . . . No . . . (*Pause. Thinks*) . . . No . . . I don't think . . . Oh, yes, do you mind if I tape over your 'Ally McBeal's'? A Jackie Chan season starts tomorrow.

CHLOE: My God, you're such an impossible prick. You're nothing but a sphincter muscle masquerading as a human being!

She exits, slamming the door behind her.

DARREN: Strange, I thought she *liked* Jackie Chan.

DR PHIBES: Well, you certainly handled that with all the sensitivity I would expect of a man who can break wind to the tune of 'The Old Grey Whistle Test'.

DARREN: (*Bursting into tears*) What am I gonna do? Chloe. What am I gonna do? I can't go on without her. (*Pause*) I've got laundry.

CUT TO–

Scene Five:
Darren sits at the dinner table with a napkin tied around his neck. Dr Phibes sits beside him.

DARREN: Thanks for coming round, Mum. I didn't know what to do.

Darren's Mum enters, carrying a large, steaming plate of food. She looks exactly like Darren, except for the fact that she is wearing a dress . . . and has breasts . . . and a perm. The goatee beard however is exactly the same.

MUM: That's alright, sweetheart. I can't have my son going without. You get stuck into this. A boy needs his mother in times of trouble.

DARREN: Thanks Mum.

MUM: We'll soon have this place shining like a new pin. After that, I'll start on your washing.

Darren turns to Dr Phibes, grinning from ear to ear.

MUM: (*To Dr Phibes*) Oh, and I haven't forgotten you either kitty. I've got you a lovely bit of smoked salmon for your tea.

Dr Phibes turns to Darren, grinning from ear to ear.

DR PHIBES: Very generous woman, your mother.

FADE TO–

Scene Six:
Darren sits on the settee, with his legs up. He is eating a large Knickerbocker Glory style dessert. His mother plumps his cushions.

MUM: Now, is everything alright, dear?

DARREN: Absolutely fine, Mummy.

MUM:	Would you like the telly on?
DARREN:	Not at the moment.
MUM:	Are you sure? Cos I got you one of those all female, naked prison videos that you like.
DARREN:	Oh, thanks Mummy.
MUM:	You're welcome, darling.

The sound of a banging door, followed by footsteps, can be heard from the flat above. All eyes turn towards the direction of the sound.

MUM:	(*Looking towards the ceiling*) Is that him? The one who stole the love of your life? The one who took your once loyal girlfriend, and introduced her to sexual pleasures she had never even dared imagine? Is this the man who brought your soul mate to a frenzied peak of erotic ecstasy, begging him to stop, yet praying he would continue. Deeper and deeper, thrusting all the—
DARREN:	(*Cutting in*) . . . Er . . . Yes, Mum. That's . . . him.
MUM:	(*Suddenly angry*) Right, I'll teach him to steal your fiancée. Nobody makes a cuckold out of my son and gets away with it. I'm gonna give him a piece of my mind. (*She starts to exit*) Oh, when I get back I'll make you a lovely dinner. And there's a nice piece of sturgeon for you as well kitty. (*Exits*)
DARREN:	That's my mum.
DR PHIBES:	Remarkably generous woman.

CUT TO–

Scene Seven:
Darren is laying in bed. Dr Phibes is sitting on the bedside table.

DARREN:	Cor, Mum's been up there a while. (*Pause*) She must be really tearing him off a strip. (*Pause*)

Boy, I'd hate to be in his shoes right now.
(*Pause*)

We hear the sound of a squeaking bed from the flat above.
Darren and Dr Phibes look up slowly.

DARREN: Oh, bollocks!

DR PHIBES: (*Pause*) Incredibly generous woman, your
mother.

FADE–

THE END.

Life–1, Bloke–Nil was created as an animated sitcom because the
likelihood of finding a cat that could handle all that dialogue was
a little slim. Of course, it could be possible to have a live action
version, with perhaps an animatronic cat – the US sitcom *Sabrina
the Teenage Witch* uses exactly this device. However, in the long
run, animation provided more freedom to create a fully rounded
character for the cat, as well as proving less costly. We make no
claims as to being experts on animation – fortunately we have
colleagues who are very talented in that particular department –
but we are led to believe that with computer graphics being what
they are, the turnover time on cartoon production is now
relatively swift. Although this is an animated vehicle about a man
and his 'superior' cat, it is simply a spin on the basic chalk and
cheese (and 'flatshare') sitcom scenario. As you go on to read the
subsequent chapters, you will find that all of the elements
discussed are in some way incorporated in the script of
Life/Bloke. At least, we *hope* you will!

Live performances

Something else to think about may be the option of having your
script performed live. Venues such as The Soho Writers' Theatre
put on seasons of short sitcom scripts, the idea being that writers
can invite producers/commissioning editors to see their work up
and running (the scripts, hopefully, not the commissioning
editors!), with genuine audience reaction, rather than on a cold
page. Channel 4's sitcom festival consisted entirely of evenings of

sitcoms staged in three's. It was out of this very process that the successful series *Black Books* was commissioned. There's nothing like a live audience to let you know whether or not your script is working, which isn't to say that if you perform it once and the response is negative, then it's no good. This certainly isn't the case. However, if you perform it for a week and the audience nod off at exactly the same point every night, well . . .

Anecdote time

Many years ago, we were involved in (to the best of our knowledge) the first and only sitcom written entirely for the stage. The Hackney Empire was the setting for this nerve shredding experience. At the time the Empire was staging a weekly variety/talent show, and someone came up with the idea to have a sitcom while the judges made their decision. So, basically, we had to write a 30-minute episode from Monday to Thursday, rehearse it on the Friday and Saturday, and perform it on the show on Sunday. The next morning we started the whole process again with a brand new episode. All in all, we wrote and performed 10 complete half-hour scripts in as many weeks. A live 'theatrical' sitcom is an absolutely amazing thing to have been involved in, but definitely not the norm. However, if you have the stamina, the rewards both short and long term, are tremendous. Being live, of course, presents ample opportunities for the insertion of topical material, as well as 11th hour rewrites, and just plain 'cuts'.

Published scripts

Also, try to get your hands on existing sitcom scripts. Many are in print and we have provided a list of several of them in the resource section of this book. You can, of course, find many scripts on the Internet. Whatever your pleasure, there's guaranteed to be a fan site somewhere, containing transcribed versions of your favourite shows. This may get a little tricky, but if you are lucky enough to get hold of a published script for an episode of something you have on tape, try reading along as you watch (or listen), and see how the published draft compares with the broadcast version. Sometimes what the producers left out can be just as revealing as what was kept in! It may also prove extremely useful if you can get along to see or hear a sitcom being recorded. If you've decided that this is the business you want to be in, it makes sense to see how the business works . . . at least on a recording day, anyway. The BBC Ticket Unit can provide you with . . . tickets, and they're free! Check our friendly, neighbourhood resource section for further information. Gosh, aren't we good to you?

Target audience/time slots

Something else to think about before actually putting pen to paper (or fingers to keyboard) is, 'What audience and time slot am I aiming for?' If, for example, you want to write a series about pensioners determined to make the most of their remaining years, reliving their teenage days and getting up to high jinks in the Yorkshire countryside, you may have a pre-watershed BBC time slot in mind, figuring that an audience of a similar age to the characters would be most likely to tune in at that time (by the way, we don't recommend you actually try and write this series, otherwise you may find yourself receiving several strongly worded letters from a Mr Roy Clarke). If, however, you decide that you want to take a less gentle approach, and intend to fill your script with expletives and full frontal nudity, then perhaps a post-watershed slot on Channel 4 is more your bag. The choice, of course, is entirely up to you, but it is a good idea to bear it in mind before you start.

As mentioned earlier in this chapter, there is a trend at the moment towards more youth orientated series, the 18–30 age range being the demographic of choice for most salivating commissioning editors, and you may feel that your idea for a series can tap into this market. In fact, you may feel that you want to take it to the extreme and write a series for children's TV. If you have never considered this option up until now, please don't be tempted to look upon it as an easy one. Children's sitcoms are just as difficult to write as those aimed at 'adults'. In fact, in our experience, perhaps even more so. Having recently been involved in the writing of a new sitcom aimed at 8–12 year olds for the BBC, we know that there are very specific do's and don'ts when it comes to writing for kids. Scenes and dialogue have to be short and snappy. This is, of course, a good rule of thumb when writing a script for any age group, but of particular importance when working on a show for kids. Shorter attention spans and all that . . . A good working knowledge of contemporary slang and popular culture is also a must. Any dialogue with references to Marty Wilde or 'Groovy happenings' is a bit of a no-no! Youth culture being the transient beast that it is, it pays to bear in mind that what's in fashion at the time of writing your script, may no longer be by the time your series is broadcast. Of course, without the aid of your scriptwriter's crystal ball, you will have no way of determining what's going to be in or out, but a script that relies heavily on a reference to a popular boy band for example, may seem a little passé when 6 months after the last full stop, members of said boy band are back stacking shelves for a living.

At the other end of the scale, there are many successful series aimed at the more mature audience. Bob Larbey, who in collaboration with John Esmonde was responsible for writing such smash hits as *Please Sir* and *The Good Life*, seems to have cornered the market as a solo writer, in 'middle-aged' romantic comedies. With *A Fine Romance* in the 80s and more recently *As Time Goes By* (both featuring the sublime Dame Judi Dench), Larbey has proven beyond a shadow of a doubt that there is an audience eager to witness, empathize with, and most importantly laugh at, the romantic involvements of ladies (and gentlemen) of a certain age. In fact, numerous aspects of 'senior' lifestyles have been mined to comic effect in recent years. *The Golden Girls*, *Waiting for God* and *One Foot in the Grave* have all dealt with the various escapades of the over-60s, and while it is certainly true to say that these series were hugely popular with audiences of all age groups, the themes and attitudes expressed would clearly resonate most with viewers of a similar age to the characters involved.

Theme music

Another aspect of sitcoms worthy of a brief mention, outside of the writing and the performances, is the theme music. While this rarely has anything to do with the scriptwriter (John Sullivan being a notable exception, having written the lyrics for the opening themes to *Only Fools and Horses* and *Dear John*), the theme music plays a hugely important role in setting the mood for a series. Consider the rinky-tink piano of *Rising Damp*, or the loping beat of *Steptoe and Son*, not to mention the sophisticated flute and almost reggae rhythm of *Shelley* or the wistful vocals to *Agony*. These all play a part in our recognition of a sitcom, and serve to create an atmosphere – think of 'Suicide is Painless . . .' from *M*A*S*H*, for example. In some cases, the theme music (or certainly the lyrics) actually aids new viewers by back-referencing the central premise of the series, as in the case of *The Fresh Prince of Bel-Air* or *The Brady Bunch*.

Chances are, when you think of your favourite sitcoms, you also think of their theme tunes, be they quirky (*Frasier*), referential (*Maid Marian and Her Merry Men*), or just plain melodious (*Robin's Nest*).

Collaboration

There is one more thing we would like to discuss before you start to actually work on your sitcom. Up to this point, we have taken it for granted that you will be embarking on your journey to sitcom writing glory on your own – which is rather a silly assumption, considering the fact that there are two of us writing the book you hold in your hand – but you may intend to work in partnership with someone else. Of course, you have to know whether or not you are compatible with your proposed partner before taking such a step as getting down to working on something as potentially time-consuming as a sitcom script. A shared sense of humour is a must (naturally), but that humour need not manifest itself in the same way for both of you. While one of you may be a whiz at a snappy one-liner, the other's strength may be in visual gags. You may come from totally different backgrounds, racially, socially, politically, sexually or even theologically (it's rather unlikely that you'll have *all* of those differences, otherwise, how did you two meet up in the first place?), but as long as you share some common ground as regards your sense of humour, you have the makings of a beautiful relationship . . . Perhaps. To paraphrase no less an authority on comedy than Bob Monkhouse 'If both partners agree on exactly the same things all the time – one of them is redundant!' Bob was responsible for co-writing the 1950s BBC sitcom *My Pal Bob* with his partner Denis Goodwin. The duo also created the 60s series *The Big Noise*, starring Bob as a brash DJ, so he knows of which he speaks! (By the way, another successful writing union, Muir and Norden wrote the series.)

Having written both solo and with other collaborators for TV, the stage and in print, we can extol the virtues and bemoan the failings of such relationships. We can vouch for the fact that writing solo can be a very lonely business, with only your ideas for company, and no one to tell you that the company you're keeping might be bad. A writer's block is a terrible obstacle to try and overcome on your own. Non-writers (from the ranks of which you are soon to be promoted) seem to think that 'writer's block' means that you can't think of anything to write at all. This isn't quite the case. When you have writer's block you can have loads of ideas . . . but they're all about as useful as chocolate teapots! To quote the master Neil Simon on the subject: 'You can think of hundreds of things. You just don't like any of them. And what you like, you don't trust!' Well, at least with a partner you can share the paranoia. However, when the ideas are flowing, collaboration is a dream situation to be in, akin to a game of table tennis . . . or at the very least, a rather lively game of draughts. There are many different approaches to collaborating on a project and it's just a question of finding the method that works for you both.

David Croft and Jimmy Perry have been cited as saying that their method of working on *Dad's Army*, was to work out the storylines to two episodes and then go away and write an episode each – two shows in half the time. Another way is to sit opposite each other and thrash out the ideas from conception to final full stop, swapping jokes, honing them, re-writing them, discarding them, until finally . . . you've come up with the working title. (We're joking, of course. This was the method we employed when we had to beaver our way through the live sitcom we mentioned earlier, and it seemed to work, we think . . .) Things like taking it in turns to do the typing, going out for sandwiches, etc are left to your own discretion. The keyword here is 'teamwork' (actually, our original keyword was going to be 'compromise' – but we couldn't agree on it!) We'll be looking at the practicalities of 'team-writing' in more detail in our final chapter. Suffice to say, whatever way you choose to write, write you must – so let's get to it!

2. Starting your Sitcom

Characters

In our opinion (and we cannot stress enough that the contents of this book are only our opinions, based on years of writing experience) the term 'Situation Comedy' is a little bit of a misnomer. What you're dealing with in the pages of your script is actually 'Character Comedy'. Of course, the situations that your characters find themselves in are important, as are things like location, time period etc, but regardless of how colourful a setting, or how outlandish or fast paced a plot, if your characters have all the believability, warmth, charm, humour and just plain personality of a soggy flannel . . . then who cares?

Take for example Richard Curtis' and Ben Elton's wonderful character *Blackadder* (deliciously brought to life by Rowan Atkinson, of course, for *'tis he* . . .). The very nature of the premise meant that with each new series (four to date, plus a couple of one-off specials) the time periods would change, allowing our 'hero' to become a relative of the previous incarnation. However, from Elizabethan, through Regency period, up to early 1900s, Edmund Blackadder (with a few subtle variations and concessions to contemporary language and fashions etc) remained his wily, cynical, Machiavellian self, reacting to each era's given set of circumstances with his customary sarcastic wit and penchant for inflicting swift, violent retribution on underlings. The point being that regardless of situation, the character was so clearly defined that the audience were/are prepared to accept the new surroundings and his place in them.

In recent years there seems to have been a trend in sitcoms that purport to be *about* very little. Almost anti-situation comedies, in a sense. *Seinfeld* billed itself as 'The Show About

Nothing'. Well, that's not entirely true, because, of course, a show about nothing would last only slightly longer than it has just taken to read about it. *Seinfeld* plots tended to deal in trivial incidents, blown out of all proportion, so while not exactly about 'nothing', they certainly did extract a lot of comic mileage out of the minutia of life. What *Seinfeld* had going for it, apart from well-written scripts, was strong characters.

The Royle Family makes an absolute virtue of the fact that the characters hardly ever leave the confines of the living room, and that the dialogue frequently pauses while the characters ostensibly just sit and watch the television. Despite containing some hilarious dialogue, the humour comes from the characterisations and the subtlety of the interaction. Series such as the brilliant and long-running *Shelley*, about an intellectual 'layabout', frequently centred on philosophical debates around the kitchen table between Shelley, Fran his long-suffering girlfriend, and Mrs H, their landlady. This wasn't exactly like *The Royle Family*, because the characters did leave the confines of the house to visit other locations, depending on the plot (an episode from a later series actually took place entirely on a tube train stuck in a tunnel), but, like *The Royle Family*, it was capable of holding the attention simply by the sharpness of the dialogue and the characterisation.

Of course, more famous examples of character over plot can be found in the work of Galton and Simpson (with a nod to Tony Hancock). 'The Bedsitter' episode from the final series of *Hancock's Half Hour* in 1960 consisted entirely of him, alone in his room, trying to decide what to do with his evening, ultimately doing nothing at all. An earlier example of this can be found in an episode from the radio half hours. 'Sunday Afternoon at Home' was exactly that – Hancock, Sid James, Bill Kerr and Hattie Jacques stuck indoors with absolutely nothing to do. For this episode, Galton and Simpson experimented with relatively long pauses, during which, the respective characters pondered their options. This was virtually unheard of at the time, and a huge risk. A character pause on screen is acceptable, because you can at least still see the character. A character pause on the radio is . . . well, just silence. (Jack Benny, the legendary American comedy star, had the stage persona of being incredibly stingy. Once, on an episode of his radio show, his character was involved in a stick-up. On being posed the question 'Your money or your life?' he famously paused for 90 seconds before replying 'I'm thinking, I'm thinking!' To quote Bob Hope, it was 'one of the biggest laughs ever heard in radio'.) The fact that the writers and performers could get away with such long pauses and plotlines that effectively went nowhere, yet still held the interest and generated massive audience laughter, is a testament to their skill and the fully defined characters involved.

We're not for a second trying to undersell the importance of any of the other components that go to make up your sitcom, far from it. We shall be looking at settings and scenarios later on, but for the moment, let's concentrate on the little darlings who are going to inhabit the world you eventually create.

Before you can write successfully for any given character, you have to have a complete understanding of what makes them tick. This may seem fairly obvious, but it's surprising how many submitted scripts fail because the writer has taken an approach along the lines of: 'Jack has a Liverpudlian accent and a stutter, therefore he is funny – job done!' Okay, so it's unlikely that anyone would really be that cut and dried about their characters, but it does serve to illustrate the point that sitcom characters, like any fictional creations, only really work when they are three-dimensional.

Most writers in any genre have likely as not experienced the following scenario: you are at a family gathering of some kind, and the subject inevitably comes up (usually raised by an overzealous elderly aunt or uncle) that you are a writer. Immediately you find yourself bombarded with suggestions from all and sundry as to jokes you can use, stories you could tell, or characters you should write about. 'My boss, now he's a real *@%$*! Miserable as sin he is! You should stick him in a show!' 'Did I ever tell you about great-auntie Phyllis . . . ? She used to dance in Paris before the war. Had a really high-pitched giggle. You should write a show about her . . . ' etc. Now, your initial reaction may be to dive under the nearby buffet table, eating yourself sick, until the familial 'think-tank' have long gone home. However, it may be useful to take your notepad under there with you, because otherwise you may just miss out on a potential fund of ideas for your script.

It's probably fair to say that all writers base their characters on people they know personally, at least in some small part. John Sullivan worked for a time in his youth on market stalls, and while he may not have met a character exactly like Del Trotter, it's more than likely that several of the people he came into contact with had certain personality traits that could later be drawn upon when the time came for Mr Sullivan to write about the Peckham impresario. However, just basing them on a real person isn't enough to make the character come alive on the page, air or screen. You as the writer have to supply the character with the humour and dynamism that will make an audience care about what happens to them and want to see more.

One trap that new writers can fall into is to try and go out of their way to create 'crazy' or 'zany' characters, chock-a-block with idiosyncrasies, in an attempt to avoid using stereotypes. Who knows, you may hit upon something, but the reality is that, whether we like to admit it or not, stereotypes are inevitable, and in many ways should be embraced. Let us qualify this. Unlike say, 30 years ago, negative racial and sexual stereotypes are nowadays frowned upon, *and a good thing too*! The very book you are reading is the collaborative effort of an Irishman and a Black man, so believe us, we've had it up to here with racial stereotypes especially.

However, social stereotypes are another matter entirely. The uptight, pedantic office manager, the opinionated cab driver, the lazy council worker, these are all stereotypes as old as the hills, and yet they are constantly reworked and included in even the sharpest of contemporary sitcoms. The trick is to find a new slant on such characters. Yes, the cab driver may be verbose and opinionated, but she may also be an Asian mother of three, with an interest in Pre-Raphaelite art. The pedantic office manager may be a gay, middle-classed Glaswegian, who has aspirations of becoming a reggae bass player. The lazy council worker, may be . . . everything you might expect a traditional sitcom council worker to be – tea drinking, tabloid reading, bum cleavage showing – but he or she may also be only four feet tall, trying to earn enough money to open their own soft furnishings business. Of course, these are slightly exaggerated examples, and your characters may be none of these things. You may decide that your cab driver is a middle-aged white male, with opinions on nothing more earth shattering than the showing of his favourite football team. The choice is, of course, yours. It is obviously your job to create characters that are believable and that you can sustain for, hopefully, many series to come. If you do try to 'play' with audience expectations, and decide to make your characters slightly 'off beat', be careful not to make them one-joke characters, with nowhere to go beyond their initial 'unexpected' character traits.

Wherever you get the inspiration for your characters from, be it real life or completely off the top of your head, they have to be clearly defined. To this end, there are several questions you have to ask about each of your characters, such as:

What is my character's defining want?

Or, put another way, 'What do they want out of life?' Every sitcom character generally has a central objective, although it need not be anything as lofty as discovering a cure for cancer, inventing a device for time travel, or achieving World Peace. Perhaps all your lead character wants out of life is to find out what they want out of life . . . It could be argued that Compo in *Last of the Summer Wine* simply wanted to have fun, although his more immediate objective was to have his wicked way with Nora Batty. Sexual desire is a prime character motivation in sitcoms – think Niles for Daphne in the earlier series of *Frasier*, Gladys Pugh for Mr Fairbrother in *Hi-De-Hi!*, and virtually every other character for anything that moved in *'Allo 'Allo*. Joey from *Friends* ultimately wants to become a successful actor, while his day-to-day objectives generally consist of getting laid and getting fed (although not necessarily in that order). Even a small supporting character like Gunther, the coffee shop manager in *Friends*, who barely speaks ten lines of dialogue per series, has a defining want – his unrequited love for Rachel. The characters in *M*A*S*H* shared the common objective of wanting to get back home safe and sound. Tony's objective in *Men Behaving Badly* was to have a relationship with Debs from upstairs. Hyacinth Bouquet's central objective can be summed up in the very title of the series she looms over: *Keeping Up Appearances*.

Whatever you decide for your characters is entirely up to you, and naturally not every script will be specifically about their aims and objectives, otherwise this will become a very one-note affair indeed. However, your character's goals in life will, in some way be reflected in their actions and dialogue, regardless of the situation or plot of a given episode. For example, Niles in *Frasier* isn't suddenly going to turn into a genuine beer-swilling, football-story-swapping, foul-mouthed lad, just because (for whatever plot conceit) he happens to be in a rough, downtown bar. Perhaps, it was a case of his trying to 'rescue' his beloved Daphne, after she has taken a job in the bar as a waitress. True, the plot may call for him to somehow pretend to be a manual labourer of some description, and Bulldog may have even given him an intensive course in 'Jock' vernacular, but Niles is a man of refinement, not to mention an outright snob. If one of the bar patrons were to pass a sexist remark about another of the waitresses, Niles' innate sense of justice would force him to chastise the man in some way. This aspect of his personality will always rear its head, ultimately scuppering the masquerade. Which leads us to another question:

How does my character react in a given situation?

Put simply, once you have created your cast of characters, your job as writer is to then throw as much trouble at them as you can, and see how they get out of it. If your characters are clearly laid out, then their reactions will suggest themselves. Let's use *Frasier* again as an example, but this time we'll take the titular character himself. Say, for example, Frasier went along to the aforementioned downtown bar in a bid to extricate Niles from, basically, getting his head kicked in. Frasier's approach, when confronted by a seven-foot bully, may well be to try and reason with the man. As a trained psychiatrist, he prides himself on his ability to communicate and reach a deeper understanding with people from all walks of life. This would inevitably create more problems than it would solve. His father, Marty Crane's approach, however, would probably be a far more straightforward, common sense, 'Buy the guy a drink and get the hell outta there!' Once you have a handle on how your characters react, you can begin playing with them, secure in the knowledge that what they do in episode 1 is what they'll do in episode 51. Predictable – no! Consistent – yes!

Having said that, it is always fun for a writer and the audience (hopefully) to play with a character's personality from time to time. An obvious example of this would be to take an essentially cowardly character and have them become brave, albeit only for the duration of that particular episode. In an episode of the series *The Brittas Empire*, pedantic, anally-retentive leisure centre manager Gordon Brittas became hypnotised, effectively changing him into an attractive, sensitive, charming man. So much so, that his long-suffering assistant Laura began falling for him. Of course, all hopes were dashed when Brittas returned to 'normal' by the end of the episode (but not before an especially poignant scene where Laura and the 'nice' Gordon have dinner and she almost reveals her true feelings for him).

Well, now that you've started to think about where your characters are trying to get to, and how they'll behave when they get there, perhaps it's time to look at:

Where does my character come from?

It's essential that you know your character's 'back story' even if you don't intend to refer to it in a particular episode or episodes. You never know when you might want to drag something up from a character's past, to smack them in the face with it in the present. Let's use *Frasier* as an example one more time (we do like other sitcoms as well, honest!) As you doubtless know, Frasier Crane was first created as a character in that other excellent sitcom *Cheers* (see, we told you we liked others), and over the course of time in *Cheers* certain aspects of Frasier's background were referred to, one aspect being the fact that his father had died. When it was decided to give Frasier his own spin-off series, he suddenly found himself reluctantly sharing accommodation with *his father*. Short of Frasier climbing into the family plot, how was this possible? Well, the subject wasn't raised until Sam, the lead character from the by now off-air *Cheers*, paid Frasier a visit on his own series many years later. Frasier dismissed the incongruity by stating to his father that the reason for announcing his death was that they had had an argument on the phone at the time, and he was in a bad mood. And the episode moved on . . . So, if even the mighty *Frasier* and his writers can come potentially unstuck (although to be fair, if the scriptwriters hadn't raised the point, it's doubtful whether anyone would have remembered Frasier's earlier paternal post mortem), it pays to have an understanding of your character's life prior to the first episode.

Did your character have a happy childhood, if so who were their best friends? Did they come from a large family or are they an only child? Were they raised by both their parents or neither? Perhaps they were raised by grandparents or an aunt and uncle. Maybe they were adopted? Did an incident occur in childhood which may somehow impact on their adult life? In an episode of *M*A*S*H*, Hawkeye Pierce was suddenly struck down by flu-like symptoms, rendering him incapable of performing surgery. After running numerous tests Colonel Potter and the rest of the medical staff could find nothing physically wrong with him, despite his very real bout of sneezing. However, when a psychiatrist was called in, it eventually came to light that the reason for Hawkeye's symptoms was far more deep seated. Without outlining the entire plot (excellent though it was), basically Hawkeye's sense memory was triggered by the damp smell of the clothes of a wounded soldier he had operated on the night before. As a child, Hawkeye's older cousin, whom he loved and looked up to, had deliberately thrown him into a lake whilst fishing, knowing that, at the time, Hawkeye could not swim. Over the years, Hawkeye had blocked the incident from his mind, not wishing to think badly of his cousin, until the smell reminded him of his own clothes as a boy. Once Hawkeye was made to confront the memory, the sneezing stopped. Oh, by the way, there were some laughs in this episode as well . . .

Think about any jobs your characters may have had prior to our meeting them. What is their educational background? Perhaps they were married. Again, entirely your call. As we say, you may not use this information straight away, or at all, but what we said about looking at other writers' existing sitcoms analytically in the last chapter, goes double for your own. Of course, where your character is from geographically, socially, or academically will probably have a bearing on:

How does my character speak?

If your character is originally from another country, this may have some impact on the way you phrase the dialogue for that particular character. Manuel in *Fawlty Towers*, for example, is from Barcelona, and has a poor grasp of English, so, obviously, if you were writing for his character, you would not give him the same kind of speech as you would, say, Major Charles Emerson Winchester, the eminent Harvard-educated, New England surgeon from *M*A*S*H*. Perhaps your character has strange vocal quirks, such as a use of malapropisms, like Del Boy Trotter in *Only Fools and Horses*. Maybe there is an unusual cadence to their speech, such as Chandler in *Friends'* habit of stressing certain words. When writing for characters with regional accents, it's useful to bear in mind the colloquialisms of that particular area. A Liverpudlian character may use the phrase 'come 'ead' rather than 'come on' for example. A Jamaican character, on the other hand would more likely ask, 'Is where you ah go?' than 'Where are you going?' (and contrary to popular belief, they wouldn't end every sentence with the term 'Mon'). It's useful, when writing characters who perhaps come from a different ethnic background to your own, to have an understanding of the way they actually speak, otherwise you may find yourself making fundamental mistakes (not to mention turning out clichéd dialogue and causing potential offence): Do all Scottish people really say 'Och aye, the noo'? Do Irish people really greet everyone with 'Top of the morning'? Do Chinese people all say 'Ah-So!'?

Even if all of your characters come from the same city, with the same ethnic and educational backgrounds, they will still speak differently. They have to; otherwise it's back to the drawing board for you, my friend. Your characters should not be interchangeable, but distinctive individuals.

Consider the script for an episode of *Sex and the City* (if you have one nearby, so much the better, but read this first!) If you pick a page of dialogue between the four central characters, and cover up the names, it will still be possible to determine who said what, just by the different ways in which the lines are written. Miranda's are the ones with the cynical, witheringly sarcastic comments, Charlotte's are the ones tinged with

35

sweetness, optimism and relative naiveté, Carrie's are the snappy, pun-tastic one-liners, and Samantha's . . . well, Samantha's are the ones most likely to make you drop your script and head for a cold shower.

When writing for your characters, they should each have their own sense of humour and ways of expressing it. Trigger in *Only Fools and Horses*, always several steps behind everyone else mentally, is a hysterically funny character, without the character himself ever trying to say anything remotely amusing, unlike Chandler from *Friends*, who is funny and he knows it, using his sense of humour as a defence mechanism. In fact, it has been pointed out before – but is worth repeating here – one of the differences between American and British sitcoms, is that in the US shows, characters laugh at each other's jokes. Next time you watch *Frasier* (there's that name again!) and Frasier passes a witty remark, look out for an exchange of smiles between Niles and Marty, or Daphne and Roz. See if we're not right.

One device used by scriptwriters to help give their characters a distinctive 'voice' is the catchphrase. Although not as prevalent in contemporary sitcoms, it was absolutely *de rigueur* for writers from the 50s to the 70s, and beyond. Think of a particular character, and it's likely that the first thing that springs to mind is their catchphrase. Whether it be Olive's whining cry of 'Oh, Arthur!' in *On The Buses*, Jacko's 'I'll have half' in *Love Thy Neighbour*, or the deadpan delight of *Rhoda's* 'Hello, this is Carlton your doorman', the writers considered it their duty to work these phrases into their characters' dialogue, much to the audience's satisfaction. While the trend for out and out catchphrases in sitcoms seems to have lessened, there are still examples of the correct use of a familiar line to be found. Let's bring Trigger from *Only Fools and Horses* back into the scene for a moment. Since 1981 he has been greeting the character Rodney with the line 'Watch 'ya Dave', to absolute gales of laughter. And rightly so, because the judgement of John Sullivan's writing and Roger Lloyd Pack's performance make it consistently funny, years after repetition should have rendered it meaningless.

Once you've considered the way your characters speak, it might be a good idea to try and figure out:

How do my characters relate to each other?

It's generally accepted that the key to any sitcom relationship is *conflict*. This can be anything from minor differences of opinion, to all out war. This conflict usually arises from characters being thrown together in an environment from which they cannot escape. We mean this figuratively, although in the case of *Porridge*, the confinement was literal. Think *Steptoe and Son* for example. A classic case of two characters with opposing outlooks, bound together by, in this case, family ties. Oh, how we longed for Harold to become immune to his father's emotional blackmail, and make a break for freedom, seeking out his little corner of the world where he could indulge in the finer things in life, such as art, literature and music – yet, at the same time, we couldn't wait for Old Man Steptoe to puncture his son's pretensions with a crass comment or gesture.

Basil and Sybil Fawlty existed in a state of mutual loathing. However, due to Sybil's domineering personality, Basil was rendered virtually impotent in her presence, causing him to vent his frustration on guests and hotel staff members. Blackadder kowtowed to the Queen but rode roughshod over Baldrick. Even though Captain Mainwaring was the superior officer in the Home Guard, and the manager at the bank, he subtly exhibited an inferiority complex towards Sgt. Wilson who demonstrated an effortless charm and air of detachment.

Perhaps the central characters are not at odds with each other at all, but instead, find a point of conflict with the outside world. *Shelley*, as created and originally written by Peter Tilbury and played by Hywel Bennett, railed against a society where his education and immense intellect seemed to count for very little. The fact that he was, for the most part, too lazy to get off his backside and do something, seemed to pass him by. There were the more specific conflicts between Shelley and his landlady, Mrs Hawkins, who considered the pontificating wastrel to be 'too clever by half', but would frequently find herself drawn into his cross-table philosophical debates. In Eric Chappell's *Rising Damp*, Rigsby (played by the brilliant Leonard Rossiter) was constantly having his pre-war values challenged by the more progressive attitudes of Alan and Philip. However, despite the generation gap, and frequent clashes caused by it, the writing subtly revealed that Rigsby seemed to have affection for his tenants and would regularly seek their advice on matters of the heart etc.

Whatever the point of conflict you decide works best for your characters, it has to be something that will generate constant and new found sources of friction. If you're lucky, several series worth! You may decide that all your central characters get on really well together, without a cross word. If that is the case, then the conflict has to be introduced by an outside force: an ex-boyfriend/girlfriend shows up out of the blue, wanting to rekindle the relationship and driving a wedge between the series' lead couple; the owner of the shop arrives, announcing that she is going to let someone go, and leaves it up to the manager to choose who to fire. How about this old sitcom staple – with a slight variation: husband arrives home, announcing to wife that he has unexpectedly invited Boss for dinner. Wife panics at last minute notice. Husband states that if all goes well, promotion is on the cards. Wife works wonders preparing meal. Husband is happy. Wife is relieved. Boss is suitably impressed. So much so, that he makes pass at wife while hubby's back is turned. Whatever you do, it is essential to the success of your script that you add a little conflict into the mix. Remember the 'old' adage (actually we just made it up):

'All hugs and no kicks, make yours a dull script!'

3. Settings and Scenarios

Okay, so you have your characters. You know what they want, where they're from, how they speak to and feel about each other. Now it's time to think about where they're going to spend their lives within your script. (We'll come to what your story is actually about in the next chapter. Don't worry, we hadn't forgotten!) Well, most UK studio sitcoms (i.e. those filmed in front of an audience) generally take place within three or four sets at the most. Budgetary limitations may dictate the possibility of outside filming – but more about that later.

At the risk of sounding like an old chocolate commercial, it makes sense to structure your scripts so that the action takes place in environments where your central characters work, rest and play. For example, if your lead character is a police officer, then it seems safe to assume that you would centre a fair portion of the action in a police station. It also follows that you would show him or her after hours, relaxing at home, so a domestic set may be required. You could also have your character knocking back a plate of chips at their favourite café, where their best friend just happens to be the proprietor. The fourth set could be used for a location specific to that episode, for example, a bank where the customers and staff are being held at gunpoint.

This is, of course, a fairly traditional set up. You may decide that you don't want to have your characters at home, preferring to focus on various locations within the workplace. Jeremy Lloyd and David Croft, the writers of *Are You Being Served?* for example, rarely strayed beyond the surroundings of Grace Bros. department store. The American police sitcom (this is becoming a theme) *Barney Miller* was situated entirely within the squad room. You may feel that you wish to place your characters in totally different environments each week, say, for example, if the lead character was a fugitive on the run. It would have to be for a crime they didn't commit, naturally . . . But that's another series!

Conversely, you may wish to have your central characters in a relatively fixed location, allowing various supporting characters to come and go around them. Roy Clarke's shop set *Open All Hours*, with Ronnie Barker as Arkwright the penny-pinching grocer, and David Jason as Granville his assistant, is a prime example of this. If your central character is a doctor, this presents ample opportunity for other characters to pass through the surgery.

In the main though, it's probably best to establish locations that are logical for your central characters to inhabit. John Sullivan's superb, but sadly short-running series *Dear John* centred on a '1-2-1' group for divorcees. This setting provided an excellent environment for Sullivan's array of diverse characters to meet on a regular and logical basis. Confused teacher John, self-obsessed and delusional Kirk, embittered Kate, dull but sweet Ralph, and the sexually frustrated group leader Louise were all characters who would never have come into contact with one another were it not for the companion-ship offered by the weekly meetings of the group.

The workplace is generally a good setting for diverse characters to congregate. It also provides a good breeding ground for conflict, not only between workers, but also staff and management, the classic 'Them and Us' situation. Consider Mr Fenner constantly trying to put one over on his all female staff of machinists in *The Rag Trade*, only to have Paddy the shop steward call for 'Everybody Out' at the merest hint of an infringement of liberties.

'Compact and bijou . . .'

Placing your characters in a confined space may seem like a good choice, and it can be, so long as you can generate enough ideas to sustain your original concept. *Porridge* by Dick Clement and Ian La Frenais was set entirely in the fictional Slade Prison, and contained all the elements of character and conflict (as discussed in the last chapter) that you could wish for. Again, this was a prime 'Them and Us' situation between prisoners and authority figures, the more specific central point of conflict being that of old lag Fletcher against hard-as-nails prison officer Mr MacKay. The show was also about youth and experience, as personified by Fletcher and his cellmate Godber, with the majority of scenes taking place in the narrow confines of their cell. As you would imagine in a prison location, there were numerous 'colourful' supporting characters who came and went during the course of the series, all finding time to pass by Fletch's cell for words of advice, to pass on the latest gossip, or to get the inside track on the toilet roll concession. In the case of *Porridge*, the relative limitations of the set and the close proximity of the performers heightened the potential for long-running conflict and character interaction.

In one of the many classic episodes from the last series of *Hancock's* (TV) *Half Hour*, Galton and Simpson decided to put Tony Hancock in a confined space, and see just how much havoc he could wreak. 'The Lift' revolved around Hancock's being stuck between floors at the BBC, having demanded to be let on as the ninth passenger in a lift designed to take only eight. Having brought about the breakdown of the lift, Hancock takes it upon himself to keep the other passengers amused until help can arrive. To say that he succeeds in doing nothing of the kind, is putting it mildly. The characters involved in the scenario included a doctor, a soldier and a vicar, and although this may sound like the opening line to a dodgy gag from an 'old school' stand-up comic's repertoire, it was, in fact, a brilliant platform for Galton, Simpson and Hancock's particular brand of character comedy, with Hancock displaying his hilariously crafted traits of pomposity, righteous indignation, braggadocio and bravado as he worked his way around the increasingly frustrated group.

Hancock himself was the only consistent character of this final series, Galton and Simpson preferring to place their hero in different settings and situations with a new set of characters each week. Other episodes in this series took place in a radio studio and a hospital ward, amongst other locations, and while it's true that the writers could have based a whole series in either of those settings (as indeed other writers have since), it's unlikely that even Galton and Simpson would try to base an entire series in a lift.

'Out there!'

Rob Grant and Doug Naylor, the writers of the excellent *Red Dwarf* series, created a whole new set of rules (well, sort of) by setting their sitcom on board a spaceship, travelling through the cosmos. The cast of characters was made up of a human being, a whiny, know-it-all hologram, a subservient android, and a half-human, half-cat fashion victim. In one memorable episode, the crew landed on a planet inhabited by historical figures, such as Elvis Presley. This was clearly not the stuff of traditional sitcom – and yet, in a sense it was, because, although Grant and Naylor made full use of their futuristic settings and sci-fi references, the basic components we've already discussed were very much in place. A diverse group of characters with distinctive personalities and humour; continuing conflicts brought about by personality clashes, perceptions of status and the necessarily close quarters of the crew; consistent central locations, i.e. the bridge, the sleeping quarters, the canteen etc, providing work, domestic and leisure environments.

Other series with relatively 'unusual' settings have included: *Lame Ducks* (rural commune); *Nightingales* (deserted tower block); *Romany Jones* (gypsy campsite); *Dusty's Trail* (Western wagon train); and, how could we forget – *Hogan's Heroes* (Nazi prison camp).

Location, location, location!

On-location filming is generally limited to a few minutes on even the most popular sitcoms. However, a sure sign of your series' success will be when you are given the opportunity to write an extended 'special'. These are generally filmed on locations outside of the usual series' setting, and tend to involve the central characters going abroad. The bigger budgets provided for these specials also justify the longer running time, with most episodes stretched from 30 to 50 minutes. Series such as *Only Fools and Horses*, and *Birds of a Feather* have proven huge ratings winners with their special 'holiday' episodes. In the 1970s, most popular UK series were given their own big screen outings: *On The Buses, Man About the House, Porridge, Father Dear Father, Bless This House, Steptoe and Son, The Likely*

Lads, Please Sir! to name a few, and, like the specials, they tended to involve the cast members heading off on an 'exotic' holiday, (*Holiday On The Buses, Are You Being Served?*) although, ironically, they tended to be filmed in English film studios, unlike the 'specials' which actually uproot the characters and film them in real locations. In our opinions, these 'special' episodes very rarely work. Taking the characters outside their usual environments and placing them in unfamiliar surroundings serves only to dissipate the comedy, with more emphasis being placed on cinematic camera angles and shots of local landmarks, than character and laughs. You may, of course, totally disagree with this opinion (we can almost guarantee that the writers of said shows will!), and our comments are in no way intended as a reflection on the high quality of the respective series. It's just that . . . well, watch the special 'London' episodes of *Friends* and we think you'll see what we mean.

. . . Where for art thou, scenario . . . ?

It was decided that we would set the 'live' series we mentioned in Chapter 1, in a mobile snack bar. The idea being that our two central characters, 'identical' twin sisters, would travel from place to place, setting up their snack bar and interacting with the various characters relating to that week's episode. The fact that the sisters had aspirations beyond the catering trade meant that we could put them in increasingly bizarre situations in pursuit of their dreams of a 'Hello' magazine lifestyle. We hasten to add that this was by no means a 'realistic' show. The mere fact that one of the sisters was played by a curvaceous actress and the other by a man in drag, should give a very quick idea of the tone. Broad comedy, puns, and a complete disregard for the fourth wall theatrical convention (allowing for some lively swipes at the band members in the orchestra pit from time to time – all scripted of course) were the order of the day. Almost a cross between a cartoon and an adult pantomime, but also very much a sitcom. From week to week we began each episode with our heroines in the central snack bar setting, before moving them on to whatever location we were using for that week's story, before returning them to the mobile snack bar at the end. Bear in mind that this was performed live on stage, so our episodes were invariably written to incorporate three scenes and (if we were lucky) two sets. Despite the obvious limitations of writing a sitcom for stage (relative lack of space being the main one), we managed to work within our restrictions, establishing a workable structure from the basic 'Beginning, Middle, End' three scene convention. If memory serves, we did occasionally stray into four and five scenes, but in the main we worked comfortably with the three.

Here is a basic scenario: in the first scene the sisters would make a decision to pursue a particular goal – let's say they wanted to become film stars. In the second (and longest scene) they would appear at a film studio ready to make a screen test for their big screen debut. On the brink of success, something would inevitably go wrong – say, one of them inadvertently killing the director (hey, it was that kind of a show!), and so they would return to the mobile snack bar (final scene) to lick their wounds, shrug off the disappointment, and get back to work, content to be serving food . . . Until the following week that is.

Of course, TV sitcom conventions probably wouldn't allow for you to write an episode with only three scenes. The average scene count per episode of *Blackadder* for example, was 15, whereas we have been involved in children's sitcoms where we were required to write twice that amount. However, that basic 1, 2, 3 approach (Establish situation, Tackle situation, Resolve situation) will certainly help you when it comes to structuring your plots – but we'll be looking at that in the next chapter.

As with our reference to stereotypes in the previous chapter, don't be afraid to work with an idea for a 'traditional' setting. You may feel that a basic living room setting works best for your story. Fine, it's your approach that will make it new and distinctive. Let's take *M*A*S*H* again as an example: in its simplest terms, this is a series set in a hospital, and it would have been quite easy to have made it about the day to day goings on of a busy surgical team in peacetime America. However, by placing that surgical team in the middle of the Korean war zone – Bingo, a fresh and unique spin! It's quite true that, had they set the series in a US hospital, the characters would probably have been fundamentally the same, with the same contrasting personalities, the same hierarchical conflicts etc, but by placing those characters in the middle of a different environment, the writers immediately added to their list of options re situations, not to mention character aims and objectives (as discussed in the last chapter). In addition, the environment in which it was set and the fact that the Korean war took place in the 1950s, (the series was made in the 70s and 80s) provided the writers with a whole other era of popular culture with which to colour their dialogue, stories etc.

Of course, *M*A*S*H* was based on the novels, and then the film of the same name, but the TV writers (Larry Gelbart being one of the creators, and a main contributor) took the source material and fashioned one of the greatest sitcoms of all time. We cannot speak highly enough of this excellent series, which so skillfully took an extremely serious premise and generated so many laughs. In fact, so adept were the writers at continually developing their characters and situations, that the series itself actually ran longer than the war in which it was set.

Bear in mind that wherever you decide to set your sitcom, the locations have to provide the characters (and you as the writer) with justifiable, logical, sustainable and consistently inspiring reasons for entering and exiting: homes, restaurants, shops, pubs, museums, hotels, airports, train stations, factories, offices, classrooms etc, all fulfill this function – telephone kiosks, airing cupboards, lifts, and the boot of a Ford Cortina, probably won't!

4. Plot and Dialogue

We did warn you at the beginning of the book that 'sitcom' writing was a lot more to do with characters than it was about 'situations'. The fact that we're up to Chapter 4 and we still haven't talked about plot, certainly proves we were serious. But we hope, now that we have finally arrived at the 'plot' chapter, you'll agree that it's a lot easier to tell interesting stories when you have interesting characters to tell them about.

Actually, if you take a good cross-section of sitcoms, both classic and contemporary, you'll see there are actually two categories of plot: there have certainly been lots of clever stories with intriguing themes, unexpected twists and surprise endings . . . but there are also many 'old favourite' stories – ranging from mistaken identity and suspected affairs to blind dates and job interviews going wrong – which crop up time and time again. Yet some of the most hackneyed plot ideas can form the basis of the most memorable sitcom episodes.

The 'Flight into Terror' plot where passengers on a plane have to cope with an unexpected emergency has been used in many comedy shows (and quite a few dramas, too). However, in the *Father Ted* episode of the same name, the scenario is given a unique twist by populating the entire plane with priests, all of whom have the quirky and individual character traits for which the show is famous. Add the nervy Father Ted, neanderthal Father Jack and the stupid-to-the-point-of-genius Father Dougal into the mix and the audience is giggling in anticipation before the flight even takes off.

In the right hands, even an apparent lack of plot can be turned to comic advantage. The classic episode of *Hancock's Half Hour* which hinges on nothing more than the title character being confined to his bed-sit for the full half hour, has been cited time and time again as a masterpiece of character comedy, and we make no apology for mentioning it again here.

If you've designed your characters properly and spent enough time getting to know them, you should be able to predict how they will react in any plot situation. You can test this out right now – pick up a recent copy of the newspaper and look at a couple of news stories, preferably ones which relate in some way to the setting or environment you have chosen for your sitcom. You may find a story about a crime which has been committed or one that was narrowly foiled, or you may read about a new invention or perhaps there's some news about a movie that is due to be released shortly. Whatever the news item, imagine it is happening in *your* sitcom environment.

If the same crime took place in an episode of your show, which characters would be outraged, which would be frightened . . . and which ones would be too self absorbed to even notice? Which one of your characters might be the one to commit the crime, perhaps even accidentally? In the case of the new invention, which of your characters would get most excited about it, and which character would immediately find a way to make a complete mess of using the new device? If the forthcoming movie is the news item you chose, do you know which of your characters would be the keenest to go and see it, and who in your cast would be most likely to hate it? Playing out all these scenarios will tell you how well you know your characters . . . and perhaps kick-start your own sitcom plot ideas.

For inspiration closer to home, you can also use real life incidents that have happened to you or people you know. In some cases, simply placing your characters into the scenario instead of the actual people involved will tip it from reality into comedy. In other cases, you'll need to take the basic incident and apply a bit of artistic license.

'What if . . . ?'

One of the most useful techniques for creating sitcom plots is to apply the 'what's the worst thing that could happen' approach. This simply involves taking an incident from life, the news or your imagination and, regardless of what actually did happen, presenting your characters with the worst possible outcome of each plot development.

Say you discover a mouse in the kitchen one day. Now, depending on whether or not you're scared of mice this incident is either of no consequence or mildly amusing in a 'you had to be there' sort of way. But when you work on it for your sitcom plot, you might decide to make things worse by having a maiden aunt, who is absolutely terrified of the creatures visit your character. Let's make things worse by having her recovering from a heart bypass, so that the shock of seeing the rat (see, it's worse already) won't just give her a jolt, it may well carry her off entirely. In fact let's really make things worse by having the escaped animal be a snake rather than a small rodent. 'What is the snake doing in the house?' Well maybe it's escaped from the local zoo or circus. No hang on, let's make things worse again – it's the very expensive but much loved pet of a boss or a girlfriend, somebody our hero or heroine can't afford to upset. So now they are not only faced with the task of preventing Auntie from dying of a heart attack when she sees the escaped beastie but also keeping said beastie in one piece until it can be reunited with its rightful owner.

There are now (at least) two distinct ways in which the plot can progress – in one the humour will come from lots of narrow escapes for the old lady or the reptile, as discovery and near death experiences are narrowly avoided. The other path the show could go down is slightly darker – either the snake or the old lady *will* meet their doom, and the comedy is derived from frantic attempts to convince bereaved relatives, pet owners or police officers who will inevitably drop by, that all is well when it very obviously isn't.

If you think that plot is getting extreme, bear in mind that a classic episode of *Blackadder* used an even wilder version of this basic plot dynamic, except in this case our heroes (or whatever word you wish to apply to Blackadder and Baldrick) managed to get the wrong person beheaded and spent most of the episode trying to hide the head in question from the unfortunate victim's wife.

As we have already mentioned, *Blackadder* is something of an exception that proves a rule when it comes to sitcom plotting. Even though the show ran for several very successful series, it was technically not the same character but one of Edmund Blackadder's many disreputable descendents that was the protagonist of each individual series. This meant that the last episode of each run of six shows could break one of the cardinal rules of sitcom plotting: whatever story you tell must be resolved by the end of the episode, and can't permanently change the basic situation of the main characters. Hence, while Blackadder and his cohorts often met a sticky demise in the final show of each series, most sitcom characters who are fired, threatened with death, inherit or lose a fortune or undergo a complete personality change in the course of an episode, are returned to their original state by the time the programme ends.

'Rolling, Rolling, Rolling . . .'

Just as it's unwise to base too many episodes on outside characters for the practical reason that it gives the regular cast less to do, and just as it makes sense to have most of the plots happen on the existing sets because new ones are expensive to build, it is not a good idea to have a plotline, however funny, which irreversibly changes or destroys the premise of the series. After all, if the war ends, the police station is sold to become a parking lot or the invisible ghost becomes visible to one and all, what are you going to do for the next episode?

Yes, we know this rule has been slightly blurred in shows like *Friends* or *Frasier*, as ongoing plotlines have been introduced into later series, but by this time the characters are usually very well established and have built up a following with the viewers who as they themselves grow, like to see their favourite characters growing along with them.

Speaking of making sure plots don't affect the basic premise of the sitcom, it's also true that the first episode of a sitcom is one of the most difficult to plot, as it usually needs to set up the premise of the sitcom. If it's a '*Man About the House/Three's Company*' scenario we need to see how the unusual flatmates get together. If it's a ghost or genie sitcom we need to see how the ghost or genie first makes itself known and to which characters it becomes attached. Whatever situation you have to bring into existence, the fact that there is usually much more story to fit in a first episode means it can be quite difficult to make it funny too. For this reason you may want to bear in mind that when pitching a sitcom project many producers like to see a sample script which is a 'typical ' episode from the middle of the series as it tends to represent the whole feel of the show much more then a first episode.

From the writer's point of view too, it's often a good idea to tackle a mid-series script first as it helps you get a handle on the characters. This means that by the time you come to write the opening episode you know them well enough to get their basic comic qualities into the half hour as well as do all the necessary plot developing. (Don't forget, though, that you can't automatically assume your viewers will see the opening episode. Every episode you write should have enough information so the viewer can pick up on the lead characters and premise enough to follow the story and get the jokes regardless of whether they have seen what has gone before.)

Another factor that is a constant, no matter which episode of the show you are writing is that you must keep the time constraint in mind when selecting and developing your plot. In the average 'half hour' sitcom you actually have quite a bit less than half an hour to tell your story. Whatever plot you set up must catch the viewers' attention in the first few minutes, keep them interested enough not to switch over during the commercial break if there is one and be wrapped up at the end in a satisfying way all in around 25 minutes. Not only that, but it must make use of all the regular characters – after all, a producer is not going to take kindly to paying actors for a series and then not have them actually do anything.

'Meanwhile, back at the flat . . .'

One way you can use characters who are not involved in the main story of your episode is to create a sub or 'B' plot which is often just an extended comedy sketch. The B plot may or may not relate to the main or 'A' plot but every time you advance the A plot (which should usually involve the main character or characters – after all those are the stars the audience is tuning in to see) you can switch to the B plot for a little variety or change of pace. The best way to practise plotting your episode is to go back to the sitcom research we asked you to do at the beginning of the book. We've already noted that when you watched your cross-section of sitcoms, you will have identified how many scenes on average each show used to tell its story. Judge also how many of these were A plot scenes and how many were to do with the B plot (sometimes B plot scenes only show up at the beginning and end of the show). Anything from six to over 20 scenes can be used, depending on the type of show.

Almost as hard as developing plot ideas in the first place is cutting them down so they can be told in the number of scenes allowed. With the increasing interest in 'team writing' in the UK you may well find yourself working on series you haven't created, and this process of analysis is very useful, not just for building your own scripts but to help you become adept at turning out scripts which are in the style and pace of someone else's original concept.

Speaking of other people's ideas, another handy source of sitcom plots is to adapt storylines and themes from other media, whether novels, stage shows or movies new and old. We are not suggesting plagiarism here of course – most writers agree that there are actually only a very small number of basic story plots anyhow, all of which constantly resurface with new characters and new scenarios giving them an appearance of freshness. For instance, the popular movie *Pretty Woman* is simply Cinderella in a different guise, while the 'buddy' movie where two unlikely characters move from mutual emnity to mutual respect is a very common one on the big and small screens.

Once you've been inspired by a particular novel or dramatic scenario, can you adapt the basic plot to suit your own script and characters? An episode of *Friends* used the buddy idea to create a scenario where Monica's friends were very wary prior to meeting her latest boyfriend as she'd had such bad luck before . . . When the new boyfriend turned up he was such a nice guy that all the friends, male and female, fell in love with him – to the point where Monica was the one who got so jealous she dumped him, leaving all her friends devastated and brokenhearted. In *The Fresh Prince of Bel-Air*, Will set out to impress his girlfriend's father by pretending to be more sophisticated then he actually was, but the dad saw through the facade and took an instant dislike to him. So Will had to reveal his true self, whereupon her father melted and they became buddies. The comedy element came into play when the situation was exaggerated to the point where his girlfriend's father was spending more time with Will than his girlfriend was, leading to a break up scene with the dad which was a very funny parody of the more usual boyfriend/girlfriend one.

A special Christmas episode of *Blackadder* combined a very well known and much used storyline – Charles Dicken's *A Christmas Carol* – with the uniquely crooked quality of the central character to turn the basic plot on its head. Instead of the usual version where the Scrooge character starts off as a miser and is transformed into a humanitarian through a series of ghostly visitations, Richard Curtis and Ben Elton's *Blackadder* begins the show generous to a fault and through being constantly ripped off is slowly transformed into the cynical snakelike character we recognise from the regular series.

If you want the ultimate seal of approval for 'plotmining', Gene Perret, one of the doyennes of American comedy writers, suggests an exercise where you watch any given sitcom, take the basic plotline and then rewrite the story scene by scene using your own setting and characters. As Gene points out, if your characters are sufficiently individual, the finished product will be completely different from the plot you started with.

However you derive your basic story idea, the best way to make it work as a sitcom plot is to break it down scene by scene. Make sure that each scene moves the basic storyline along, and bear in mind that each scene must be relatively short and sharp. It can help to write out your individual scene breakdowns on index cards rather than on one sheet of paper. Then you can move things around if you need to. In particular, it can be helpful to shift your B plot scenes around to pace things a bit (you can take out one to speed things up a bit if you need to).

Even though sitcoms usually only have one commercial break in this country – and none if they are on radio or on the BBC – they follow the classic 'three act' structure. Act One sets up the 'status quo' – in other words where the main character is at right now – and then introduces the challenge or change the character will face in this episode. Sometimes the challenge is an outside occurance like a debt problem or a new relationship (it doesn't necessarily have to be negative). Sometimes it is an internal issue like a loss of confidence or worry about middle-age. Act Three is the plot resolution where whatever challenge we set up in Act One is resolved. Hopefully, regardless of whether the challenge is internal or external, the resolution will grow logically out of some action by the main sitcom characters . . . a contrived ending, or worse, the 'it was all a dream' cop-out is to be avoided at all costs. So what about Act Two? Well this is the bulk of the script, the journey from challenge to resolution and as this is a sitcom it's your job as a writer to make this journey as interesting and amusing as possible. It's in Act Two that you have to keep using the 'What's the worst thing that could happen?' technique to continually up the ante so the viewer is as anxious as the characters are to see how the plot turns out in the end.

'Speech! Speech!'

Of course there is one other big challenge for the new sitcom writer. During the writing process you can set out your plot clearly in a step-by-step outline on index cards (or at least you can after crossing out lots of cards, changing the order of others and sometimes restarting the whole thing from scratch as your characters take on a life of their own and move the story in a direction even you didn't intend!) But that's not the way the viewer will receive the information you are trying to communicate: sitcom is all about character, and the way the characters communicate with each other and the viewer is not through description but through action and dialogue.

How do you write effective, vibrant funny dialogue for your characters? Well it comes back to how well you know your characters. (We know we keep harping on about this point, but it really is the key.) The simple rule to bear in mind is that just as your characters will act differently in any given situation, they will speak differently too. Depending on their age, race, background, education and attitudes they will communicate and comment on exactly the same plot developments using radically different words, phrases and inflections – maybe even developing their own catchphrases. (See Chapter 2.)

Just as you can be inspired to write your own plots by studying the different plots that other writers have come up with, your fastest route to writing original character dialogue is to become a 'dialogue detective', cultivating a keen ear for the way different people communicate in real life. The most obvious mark of a beginner is having all the characters in a script sound alike when they talk (and quite often talk in exactly the same way the writer does). It follows then that the mark of a good dialogue writer is when you are able to cover the character names on a script and know who is speaking just by looking at the dialogue alone.

Oh, and if you do put some time into listening to how people talk, one of the things you'll notice is that by and large one of the things they don't do is talk in jokes constantly. Yes, you are writing a situation comedy and the viewers will expect funny lines, but just as action grows out of character, humorous dialogue comes from character too. In fact if your characters are strong enough, you'll find the very fact that they communicate in different ways will lead to humour when they talk to each other – in much the same way as most of the misunderstandings and conflict in real life comes from the fact that we all have different communication methods.

Gripping plot ideas, a cast of funny and endearing characters, sparkling, realistic dialogue, and all needing to be squeezed into less than half an hour. By now you may be feeling that it's nigh on impossible to get all the elements of a sitcom right. Well, it is . . . at least if you expect to get it right first time, which is why professional sitcom writers don't even try. Instead we try to brainstorm as many different plotlines and lines of dialogue as we can, knowing that the more we try out and the more we discard, the closer we are to producing the best and funniest story possible. In the last few chapters we've been looking at the individual building blocks of your sitcom. Now it's time to start working on the building. So, remembering that a building site is by its nature a messy place, turn to the next chapter and join us in the wonderful world of drafts and rewrites. It's time to get our hands dirty.

5. The Finished Article (?)

Ticking the laughs!

If you have considered all the elements we have discussed so far, applying them to your own work, you should have come up with something resembling a sitcom script. In the following chapters, we will be looking at selling your script, as well as working through the various drafts to get your work to the peak of perfection . . . but for the moment, let's look at the script as it stands.

Both you and your partner (if you have one) will have read and re-read your script many times, toying with lines of dialogue to get them 'just right'. From our own experience, we know that there may be a line that remains 'sticky'. A phrase that, try as you might, you just can't get to work the way you want it to. Then, suddenly, when you were not even thinking about it, the correct wording will present itself. Hopefully this epiphany will occur before you send the script 'off to market', but, as we will explore later, you'll probably have ample opportunity to fix it if this is not the case.

What we and many writers like to do, is to sit down with our script, taking a pencil and going through a process known as 'ticking the laughs'. This is exactly as it sounds: we've all heard the expression 'a laugh a minute', and while this is usually meant to indicate something that is positively jam-packed with laughs, in the case of a sitcom script, a laugh a minute is a pretty poor average. Considering that a sitcom for the BBC is 28 minutes long, a 'laugh a minute' script for that particular broadcaster will contain precisely 28 laughs!

As we suggested in Chapter 1, take another look at one of your favourite shows, and count the laughs in each scene. For example, in *Friends* even a 'quickie' scene, (generally used in US sitcoms), which tends to be a snatch of dialogue designed to remind the viewer of a subplot, while at the same time covering a time lapse in a larger scene, consists of at least two or three laughs in the space of 20 seconds.

While your script should by no means be just a collection of jokes strung together, we must never lose sight of the fact that the primary function of your script (and hopefully your series) is to make the audience laugh – *first and foremost*.

Taking into account the fact that an A4 page of dialogue generally translates into about a minute of screen or air time, you should be hoping for at least five laughs per page, or every 12 seconds approximately. True, you can't be quite as precise about it as that – in some cases you may have more, in others, less – but it's a pretty good target. This will take your laugh tally from 28 to 140 per episode. Sounds considerably healthier, doesn't it? This is where the process of 'ticking the laughs' comes in. If you go through your script and find that during the course of three pages, you have ticked only four laughs, then there is a problem that needs to be resolved. Although, of course, when we say 'ticking the laughs', we really should say 'ticking the jokes', because, after all, laughter is down to the audience – the reason for the laughter is down to you.

There are going to be instances when a line that has you in absolute hysterics, falls flat when delivered in front of an audience. Why this is, we do not know, and you can never fully prepare for it. Conversely, there may be a line that you think will produce nothing more than a chuckle at best, which is greeted with absolute gales of laughter, leaving your intended 'big joke' to be met with an anti-climactic 'tee hee'. With the 'ticking the laughs' approach, you will at least have a fair idea of where your laughs, big and small, are intended to be.

Then, of course, there will be lines that you had no intention of getting a laugh with, which will suddenly become hilarious due to the performer's delivery. This is a situation you cannot legislate for when at the strictly 'written' stage of your script. If your script is commissioned, and you have a particular performer in mind for a part, and if you are lucky enough to get that performer, then of course you can start to write dialogue to suit that individual performer's style. (Many years ago, a viewer wrote in to the *That's Life* programme – not a sitcom, we know, but bear with us – stating that he had an uncontrollable response to the word 'flannel'. Whenever he heard this word, he would collapse in a fit of giggles. The team decided to put this statement to the test by inviting Les Dawson on to the show to say the aforementioned word. When the viewer was confronted by Les and 'that word', the viewer was in absolute hysterics. However, Les' routines failed to provoke more than a smile from the viewer, despite the guffaws of laughter from the rest of the audience.) Anything the actor brings to your script is a bonus, but the majority of the work must be done by you on the page.

In our careers, we have been extremely lucky to have our words spoken by some very fine actors indeed. Below, we have included a sample episode of a radio series where we were given the opportunity to work with a 'wish list' of performers. This was written in very rare circumstances. The producer was already familiar with our work, and as such, simply asked us to write a script without having to go through the usual process of proposals, outlines, treatments, character breakdowns etc (we shall be looking at these in detail in a later chapter) which isn't to say that our first version of the script was the one we recorded. Far from it. We still went through several rewrites before going in front of an audience. However, once the script was completed, he simply asked us who we wanted to be in the pilot, and then set about hiring them. We hasten to point out, this is by no means the norm, but for us, just a very fortunate situation to have been in.

As you read through the script, make a note of all the rules and methods we employed, as discussed in the previous chapters. Bear in mind that this version was simply the first draft, and while not drastically different from the recorded version, there were several instances of lines having to be cut and scenes reshaped. We are aware of many 'mistakes' in this version of the script: some were identified when we 'ticked the laughs', others when the script was first read by the actors, with supposedly funny lines being met with blank expressions and stony silence. Many were simply spotted once we had left the script for a day or two and come back to it with a 'fresh pair of eyes'. For example, in Scene Three, the character 'Vi' states that the following Saturday is her Ruby wedding anniversary, by way of an excuse for not going to dinner with another man. This all seemed very contrived until we made reference to the anniversary in Scene Two during Vi's conversation with Bernadette. Suddenly the anniversary seemed not quite so 'out of the blue' when mentioned later.

Rather than present you with a polished 'final' draft, we have decided to show you this warts and all version, so as to give you some idea of just how much work you have to put into an initial script, as well as how much work there may potentially be left to do. However, bear in mind that this was the script the actors agreed to get involved in, and as such, was the version we heard when we all met for that first read through.

Do Nothing 'Til You Hear From Me

A situation comedy for radio

By Marcus Powell & John Byrne

Pilot Episode: *'Life and Soul'*

OPENING THEME AND ANNOUNCEMENTS, FADE TO–

Scene One: The Hen and Pewter Public House.

F/X: GENERAL PUB ATMOSPHERE, OVER WHICH–

ROY: Well, here's to him. We raise a cup of good cheer to one whose like we shall never see again. Cheers.

GEORGE: Cheers. Nicely put, Roy. Nicely put.

ROY: Well, George, 'Rusty' was a decent sort of a bloke, he deserves to have a few well-chosen words spoken about him.

GEORGE: You're right.

ROY: Rusty Garner was a fine man and a fine musician. Even in later years, he could still keep a beat as steady as the rock of Gibraltar. I can see him now, left foot bangin' away on the bass drum like a piston, his drumsticks a blur. Little arms whirlin' 'round like an arthritic windmill.

58

GEORGE: True, not many 72 year-old drummers around.

ROY: There's one less now. If you ask me, I say it was retirement that killed him, y'know.

GEORGE: You reckon . . . ?

ROY: Of course. 'A musician makes music – always'. Once his wife made him hang up his sticks, well . . . his 'Samson' was well and truly Delilah'd.

GEORGE: Yeh, but what about us? I mean, yeh, we're not officially retired, but we haven't worked in a while either, but we're alright. Touch wood.

ROY: Are we George? Are we really? A man can only watch so much Gloria Hunniford on daytime telly before he has to lash out. I don't know about you, fella, but I'm goin' stir crazy.

GEORGE: Well . . . It was a nice touch them laying his drumsticks on his chest in the coffin like that. He'll be able to tap out a beat for St Peter at the Pearly Gates, now.

ROY: Yeh . . . Stickin' the cymbals between his legs was a bit much, though . . . Still, a cat's last request is his last request.

GEORGE: I thought it was very moving, the way his daughter sang at the service wasn't it?

ROY: Actually, I thought she was a bit flat in the second verse to be honest. Her vibrato left quite a lot to be desired as well!

GEORGE: Roy!

ROY: Well . . . If she's gonna sing in public, she might as well come prepared.

GEORGE: Blimey, the poor girl wasn't auditioning, Roy. She was at her father's grave, singing his favourite song.

ROY: It wouldn't be if he could've heard that version.

GEORGE: Don't come it with me, Roy Walcott. I've known you too long to be taken in by this Ebenezer

Scrooge act. I saw you wiping away a tear with your sleeve.

ROY: I had to – my *hanky* was stuffed in my ears!

GEORGE: Well, you can say what you like, I only hope there's someone there to sing my favourite song when I go.

ROY: You don't have to worry about that, old fella. Of course there will be somebody there . . . You can pay people to do that sort of thing.

GEORGE: I meant a loyal family member or friend. Someone who cares enough to show a little sympathy at my passing.

ROY: Well . . . I'm sure you'll be able to find . . . someone.

GEORGE: (*Wounded*) Marvellous, and there was I thinking that you were gonna volunteer. I see that the statute of limitations on lifelong friendships runs out the moment one of you pops your clogs.

ROY: Alright, if I'm around, I'll sing at your funeral. Happy now?

GEORGE: What do you mean 'If you're around'? Are you saying you wouldn't come?

ROY: No, it's just that I'm more likely to go first, that's all.

GEORGE: Why do you say that? We're both the same age, more or less. Both at the same level of fitness, which is to say, not at all. What makes you think you'll go before I do?

ROY: Well, let's face it George. You're a pianist. You've spent your whole career sitting down, takin' it easy.

GEORGE: Oh, please Roy, not this again.

ROY: All you've had to do for the past fifty years is wiggle your fingers. The most strenuous thing you ever do is close the lid. Now me, I'm a trombonist. That's an instrument you have to put your whole body into. Your lungs, your heart, your back, your shoulders. I'm 69 years old, man. That kind of stamina is in short supply nowadays. You have to work, you have to sweat, you have to be Victor Mature to play the trombone, y' understand. You have to be John Wayne, Burt Lancaster, Johnny Weissmuller to play the trombone. To play the piano, all you have to be is . . . Charles Hawtrey! You can go on tinkling the ivories 'til the cows come home, but me . . . ? All I have to do is get over-excited during a chorus of 'New York, New York', and it's 'Come in No. 4, your time is up!'

GEORGE: If you feel that way about it, maybe *you* should retire, before it's too late.

ROY: How dare you? 'A cowboy dies with his boots on' . . . or in my case, 'emptying his spit valve'. No, I wanna go out swingin', not like old Rusty.

GEORGE: At least you've got a family to make sure you'd get a proper send-off. Look at the motley collection that's in here. Everybody sitting round looking morbid.

ROY: Oh, I see, you were expecting one of those funerals with the gymnastics display thrown in . . . ?

GEORGE: No, you know what I mean. You'd have thought that with all the people Rusty played with over the years, at least a couple of celebrities would have paid their respects.

ROY: What do you mean? Look over there by the guacamole dip, it's that bloke from the Acker Bilk tribute band. He doesn't turn out for just any old wake, y'know.

GEORGE: Yeh, well, him not withstanding, it doesn't seem like much of a tribute, to me.

ROY: Well, there's not many of the old gang around anymore. Look at old Charlie Wicksmough over there. In his day he was the toughest tenor sax man this side of the States, now look at him. He hasn't even got enough strength to lick his own roll-up.

GEORGE: Very sad.

ROY: I tell you Georgie boy, we're a dying breed . . . Literally. By the time we go, there'll be nobody left to care, believe me.

GEORGE: What about your Mrs, and your daughter?

ROY: I might as well be in the ground already, for all the attention they pay to me. You know my daughter hates my guts, and on top of that, she's a vegetarian.

GEORGE: How's your Mrs getting on with them evening classes you were telling me about? 'Literature appreciation', isn't it?

ROY: Something like that. She's still going. She was trying to tell me about it last night, but I couldn't give her my full level of concentration. I was doing a little night studying myself at the time – 'Baywatch' was on cable.

GEORGE: 'Literature Appreciation.' I think that's very commendable at her age. You see, it's never too late Roy. Never too late. I used to love literature when I was at school: 'St Agnes Eve, Ah bitter chill it was. The owl for all his feathers was a-cold, and the hare limped trembling through the frozen grass'. One of my favourites that was. Keats. You looked surprised that I can recite poetry.

ROY: I'm still surprised that you went to school!

GEORGE: Maybe you should take up a class as well.

ROY: Don't be ridiculous fella! I'm a grown man! What the hell would I be doin' goin' into school? If my wife wants to run 'round like a teenager, that's her business, but not for me. I tell you, she treats the house like a hotel. She's off first thing in the morning, then you don't see her again until the night. If it's not books, then it's afternoon tea dances with her friends, or life drawing or whatever.

GEORGE: Ooh, I could go for some of that. I quite fancy the idea of sketching some young dolly bird, all 'alfresco' like.

ROY: You'd be bloody lucky! She brought home a drawing of some bloke that was modelling the other night. Looked like Orson Welles with a bad case of mumps!

GEORGE: Still, at least she's keeping busy.

ROY: She can stay at home if she wants to be *busy*! I can keep her *busy*! All she did was nag me for years about giving up the travelling, playing in different clubs every night, and spending more time at home. Well, now I'm home, she's off – galavanting like a Wildcat of St Trinians. It's not right . . . It's wrong!

GEORGE: 'A woman doth possess myriad traits, enchanting to the eye, bewitching to the mind, and perplexing to the soul.'

ROY: More Keats?

GEORGE: No, actually that was a little something of my own. 'A George Merriman original', you might say.

ROY: Alright, I think that's enough Red Bull and Guinness for you.

GEORGE: Maybe I should take a literature appreciation class as well.

ROY: No, I think you've peaked. Actually though, maybe that's not such a bad idea at that. If you went along to this class, you could keep an eye on her, see what's so fascinating about this literature business she'd rather spend her time there, than at home with a torrid hunk of man flesh such as myself.

GEORGE: Come off it, Roy. I'm not goin' to spy on your wife. Violet's a friend of mine as well y'know. I'm sure she's just catching up on all the things she never had a chance to do when she was younger, that's all.

ROY: Is that so? I see . . . First you think you're the new Poet L'Oreal, and now you're Marje bloody Proops! Is there no beginning to your talents . . . ?

GEORGE: You know I'm right.

ROY: Well . . . never mind all that. We're here for a funeral, remember? This is Rusty's time.

GEORGE: True enough. When did they say they wanted all the musicians to play?

ROY: Just after his daughter's speech. That's a good time too, cos if she starts to sing again, at least we can drown her out.

GEORGE: Well, at least he'll have some mates playing him off. He'd have liked that.

ROY: Yeh, Rusty lived for his music.

GEORGE: We all do, Roy. We all do.

GRAMS: 'WHEN THE SAINTS GO MARCHING IN'.

Scene Two: Bernadette's house, two days later.

F/X: DOORBELL RINGING. SOUND OF DOOR BEING OPENED.

BERNADETTE: Mum. What a surprise. What are you doing here?

VI: Just a visit. I'm on my way to evening class. Made a few biscuits. I thought that you and the kids might like some . . . Oh, and I was on the verge of murdering your father with an egg whisk!

BERNADETTE: Oh. (*Pause*) Cup of tea?

VI: Thanks. He and George are at the house, rehashing the old days. Ever since that funeral on Tuesday, all he does is moan about the past. I don't mind the occasional stroll down memory lane, but your father wants to buy land and set up house there.

BERNADETTE: Sounds like Dad's got a dose of the old 'Mortality Blues'.

VI: Well, he's got nothing to worry about on that score. When the Grim Reaper comes to the door, your father will probably bore him to tears about the time he played with Cleo Laine, or something. Poor old Reaper won't stand a chance. He'll be begging to go back empty-handed.

BERNADETTE: Thanks for the biscuits. They look delicious.

VI: Oh, they're not all for you. I made a few for Alastair . . . Professor Kingsley . . . The tutor of my literature class.

BERNADETTE: (*Suspiciously*) I see . . . 'Alastair' . . .

VI: What?

BERNADETTE: (*Teasing*) Oh, nothing. I just thought that apples were the usual bribe of choice for schoolgirls trying to curry favour with teacher.

VI: Do you mind? I am doing nothing of the sort. I just happened to mention in class last week that I enjoyed baking, and Alastair said he would like to try one of my biscuits, that's all.

BERNADETTE: (*Chuckling*) I'm sure he did. So what does this Romeo professor look like then, Mum? I bet he's all greying and distinguished. I have visions of a geriatric sex bomb, brushing biscuit crumbs off a still virile moustache, seductively thumbing his dentures back in place . . .

VI: Alright, stop it right there!

BERNADETTE: Mum, I'm only teasing.

VI: Well . . . It's just that I've had to put up with the Spanish Inquisition from your father about this already. I came here to get away from the noise.

BERNADETTE: What's tugged his leash this time?

VI: Oh, you know your father. More of his usual.

BERNADETTE: Still thinks the world revolves around his rheumatism . . . ?

VI: Exactly. He can't get it into his head that I have things I want to do, while I still have the where-with-all to do them. Your father is just content stuck in front of a blasted western on the TV, or getting drunk with his musician cronies. His ambition has clotted.

BERNADETTE: Well, he is an old man now, Mum. He's set in his ways. It's to be expected, isn't it . . . ?

VI: Your father was set in his ways when he was 25. I'm still young . . . inside, where it counts, but your father can't see that . . . or doesn't want to.

BERNADETTE: So what are you going to do?

VI: Nothing . . . What can I do? Your father is . . . your father, there's no changing him, so that's that.

BERNADETTE: (*Frustrated*) Change the record can't you Mum!

VI: What d'you mean?

BERNADETTE: Your relationship is not normal. It's common-place, but definitely not *normal*. Going to the classes and stuff is a great start, but you have to do more. So many women of your age are in your situation. Living with a person they no longer love, or have anything in common with, but stick with because they think that's their lot. You said yourself, you're still young, so move on.

VI: It hurts me to hear you talk like this, Bernadette. Your father is a good man, really.

BERNADETTE: Listen, Mum, I know I might come across as a bad self-help book, but you deserve better, that's all I'm saying. I just want you to be happy, that's all.

VI: I know, darlin'. Me too, but you and I are looking at this thing from different sides. You only see your father as he is now, but I remember the man I married. Grinning on the bandstand, all cocksure swagger and Old Spice. When he played that trombone, he could charm you, y'know, really charm you. He had a way of looking at you when he spoke . . .

BERNADETTE: You mean without belching halfway through a sentence . . . ? Amazing!

VI: He was a different man then. Very different.

BERNADETTE: And you think *that man* might still be *in there* . . . ?

VI: I don't know . . . but sometimes you just want a kind word now and then, y'know?

BERNADETTE: Yes, Mum, I know.

VI: I'm too old to be swept off my feet, but a little appreciation, a smile. Not too much to ask, is it?

BERNADETTE: Not at all. In fact, I think a show of appreciation might be worth a biscuit or two.

VI: Excuse me.

F/X: DOOR OPENING.

VICTOR: Oh, hi Violet. I thought I heard your voice. How's my favourite mother-in-law?

BERNADETTE: You talk as though you've got more than one.

VICTOR: Ah . . . Well, I've been meaning to speak to you about that . . . Ow!

BERNADETTE: (*Deadpan*) Ha, ha. Roll your sleeves up, funny man. You can help me peel some potatoes for dinner.

VICTOR: Yours to command, oh great and beauteous one.

VI: I'm fine thank you, Victor.

VICTOR: Good. And how's Mr Walcott?

VI: Same as usual.

VICTOR: Oh . . . Is that good or bad?

VI: He's fine. Listen, I'll let you two get on with fixing your dinner. I'm off to my class. Say hello to the kids for me when they come home.

VICTOR: Oh, they're already here. They heard your voice but they didn't want to come down because they thought that Mr Wal– Er . . . They've got lots of homework.

BERNADETTE: Victor, can you have a look in the cupboard under the sink?

VICTOR: What am I looking for?

BERNADETTE: Nothing, I just want you to put your head in the cupboard under the sink.

VI: It's alright, you two. I'm off.

BERNADETTE: That's right, you don't want to keep Alastair waiting.

VICTOR: Who?

VI: Professor Alastair Kingsley. My Literature class tutor.

VICTOR: Are you serious?

BERNADETTE: Why, have you heard of him?

VICTOR: Yeh! Alastair Kingsley. In the 60s he was hailed as the great new voice of literature. When I was at uni, his books were like currency.

VI: Really?

VICTOR: Oh yeh. Funny, scary, profound, you name it, Kingsley had a way of blending all those elements into his work.

BERNADETTE: 'Thank you, Melvyn Bragg.' Now, there's a couple of profound King Edwards with your name on them! Get peeling!

VICTOR: Seriously, Violet, you're very lucky to be tutored by the great man himself.

VI:	Well I certainly didn't know all of that.
BERNADETTE:	Well, looks like the 'great man' has taken a shine to my 'Great Mother'.
VI:	Oh, shush.
VICTOR:	You could do a lot worse Violet. Apparently he's loaded.
VI:	(*Laughing*) You children are disgraceful. I'm a happily marri– Oh, give me my biscuits!

GRAMS: 'PLEASE BE KIND' BY ELLA FITZGERALD AND ELLIS LARKIN. LINK TO–

Scene Three: Literature class, that night.

DAPHNE:	(*Middle-aged cockney*) Here, Violet, that was a good one tonight, wasn't it? I enjoyed that.
VI:	Yes. 'A Room of One's Own'. I must admit I've never read any Virginia Woolf before, but Professor Kingsley makes it come alive to you.
CLIFTON:	(*Upper-middle class, Brian Sewell type*) Well, of course, that is his unique skill, isn't it? His oration possesses an almost supernatural intensity. A vibrancy born of a love of the written word at its most expressive, don't you agree?
DAPHNE:	Well, you certainly said a cravat-ful there, Clifton.
CLIFTON:	Quite.
DAPHNE:	You coming to the pub for a swifty, tonight, Vi?
VI:	Well, I shouldn't really . . .
DAPHNE:	What's the matter? You've always got somethin' else to do. What you up to, you saucy old minx?
VI:	I . . . I don't know what you mean. I . . .
ALASTAIR:	(*Approaching*) Er, Violet, could I have a quick chat before you leave?
VI:	Of course, Professor.

DAPHNE:	We'll get yours in, Vi. See you there. G'night Professor K.
ALASTAIR:	Goodnight, Daphne. Well done tonight.
CLIFTON:	Goodnight, Professor. A mesmeric class, as always.
ALASTAIR:	Thank you, Clifton. You are *too* kind.
DAPHNE:	Let's hope so, he's gettin' the drinks in. Come on, Clifton. I've got a thirst of almost 'supernatural intensity. A vibrancy born of a love of G&T at its most alcoholic.' Shall we . . . ?

F/X: DOOR CLOSING.

ALASTAIR:	Violet, I just wanted to thank you for the biscuits. It was very thoughtful of you.
VI:	Well, I was baking anyway, y'know . . .
ALASTAIR:	No, it was very nice. I shall enjoy them in front of the fire tonight, with a nice cup of tea. And while I savour the warmth, I shall think of you, Sweet Violet.
VI:	Alastair, please, somebody might hear you.
ALASTAIR:	So? Let them.
VI:	I don't want anyone to get the wrong idea.
ALASTAIR:	I'm sorry, Violet. Forgive me. Perhaps we can go to my house and–
VI:	Now you're getting the wrong idea. Look, Alastair, it's been really nice your taking me to tea after class these last few weeks. And I've enjoyed meeting you for coffee at the bookshop at the weekend, and I'm so flattered that you've been paying me all that attention in the tea breaks during class, but I just don't feel we should take it any further.
ALASTAIR:	Is that sentiment from your head . . . or your heart?
VI:	It's from my bladder! I'm convinced it's gonna collapse under the strain of all that tea and coffee.

ALASTAIR: (*Laughing*) Violet, Violet, Violet. Your sense of humour is one of the myriad things I find so delightful about you. I may have been a widower for the past ten years, but I do know something about women. I know you wouldn't have spent this much time with me if you weren't interested in me too.

VI: Well, I must confess, it's nice to be appreciated as a woman.

ALASTAIR: But you are no ordinary woman, Violet. Don't you see? You're . . . you're my literary goddess!

VI: Now hold on a minute . . .

ALASTAIR: I want to be the Romeo to your Juliet. The Heathcliff to your Cathy. The Pheobus to your Esmerelda.

VI: And what about Roy?

ALASTAIR: Ah, the Quasimodo to your Esmerelda . . .

VI: Alastair! My Roy is no Quasimodo.

ALASTAIR: Really? From what you tell me, he's deaf to your aspirations, the bells of complacency ringing in his ears . . .

VI: Look, Alastair, I need to think. This is too much for me. I'm leaving.

ALASTAIR: Shall we meet at the weekend, as usual?

VI: No, I mean I'm leaving the class.

ALASTAIR: What . . . ?

VI: I'm sorry, Alastair. I shall miss . . . coming here.

ALASTAIR: And Tony Bennett . . .

VI: Excuse me?

ALASTAIR: Tony Bennett. You mentioned that he was one of your favourite singers. You know he's playing the West End on Saturday? Well, I've got two tickets, so I was wondering . . .

VI:	If you think you can sway me with tickets to Tony Bennett . . .
ALASTAIR:	Of course not. I was thinking tickets, then dinner . . . And I'd get around to swaying you at the dance they're having at the Waldorf later on. You like dancing, don't you?
VI:	I love dancing . . . or I used to. Oh, Alastair, it . . . it sounds lovely, but I can't. Saturday is our Ruby wedding anniversary. It just isn't right.
ALASTAIR:	It certainly isn't. Forty years married to a Luddite like that! It's unthinkable . . .
VI:	I married Roy for better or worse. If I hang around long enough, the 'better' bit has to turn up sooner or later. Alastair, it's been nice knowing you, and thank you for your . . . very kind offer. But this is goodbye.
ALASTAIR:	Violet, wait . . .

F/X: DOOR CLOSING.

GRAMS: 'THE FOLKS WHO LIVE ON THE HILL' BY PEGGY LEE. LINK TO–

Scene Four: Roy and Vi's house, the following day.

F/X: FRONT DOOR OPENING, FOLLOWED BY–

ROY:	(*Scream*)

F/X: CRASH AND THUD OF ROY TRIPPING OVER.

VI:	(*Calling off*) What happen'?
ROY:	I nearly kill' meself tripping over these 'French Shooey' books of yours.
VI:	It's 'Feng Shui' Roy.
ROY:	Well throw it out, it's cluttering up the place!
VI:	That's what I'm doing. I'm giving that whole pile of books to the charity shop.
ROY:	Charity begins at home . . . Not that you'd know that, you hardly spend any time here since you joined that book class.

VI: Well, then you'll no doubt be over the moon to hear that I have decided to leave the class.

ROY: What? Oh, well done Vi. Well done. You finally begin to see sense. What happened, all of those young, intellectual student types making you feel about as welcome as a lobster in a Jacuzzi?

VI: Actually, no Roy. For your information, that class was good for me. For the first time in my life, I was learning things. I was growing as a person.

ROY: And I've been shrinkin' as a person. After six weeks cookin' pot noodle for meself, I can hardly keep my trousers up. But Vi, if those books mean so much to you, I'd never want you to give them away . . .

VI: Well, thank you, but–

ROY: No, if you bring them down to that second-hand shop in the market, you can get enough cash to buy me some egg fried rice on the way back home.

VI: (*Stunned*) You are so insensitive!

ROY: No I'm not! There'll be enough change for you to get yourself a spring roll.

VI: That's exactly the kind of comment that Alastair said–

ROY: Alastair? Who's Alastair?

VI: Alastair . . . Alastair Maclean . . . He wrote spy novels and things . . . We studied it in class . . .

ROY: You see? Foolishness! Reading about people sneaking round and whispering, and all that secret romance business. Nothing to do with real life!

VI: (*Quietly*) You'd be surprised.

ROY: What?

VI: You're right, it's true.

ROY: Real life is about getting through one day at a time.

VI: (*Reflecting*) One day at a time. Before you know it, it's forty years. Just like us.

ROY: Forty years . . . ? Oh, yes . . . I forgot . . .

VI: Why doesn't that surprise me? You are the most–

ROY: (*Smug*) I forgot to tell you that on Saturday night we're going out. Tony Bennett's playing the West End. I thought we might go down and see him. Apparently his brass section is meant to be pretty decent.

VI: T-Tony Bennett?

ROY: Yes, and after that, I thought we might stop off for some dinner. You know, push the boat out a bit.

VI: And afterwards, can we go dancing at The Waldorf?

ROY: 'The Waldorf'. . . Well, we'll see. I said push the boat out, not throw me pension book overboard . . . But, it's a special night, so maybe you will see a bit of fancy footwork, after all . . .

VI: Oh, Roy . . .

ROY: When we get to the Waldorf, you fake an angina attack, I'll sneak through the cloakroom, and I'll let you in the fire exit when the fuss dies down.

VI: Sounds like the honeymoon hotel all over again.

ROY: Well, only the best for my girl.

VI: It's been a while since we went out together. Saturday's going to be wonderful. I'm touched that you remembered, Roy.

ROY: Good. And I'm glad that you're leaving that class. All that education was twisting your mind, changing you. I felt like I had to go through the encyclopaedia just to ask you if you'd wash me drawers! At least when you're ignorant, I know where I stand. I may not be a big reader Vi, but our anniversary . . . ? Well, that's something I would have to be a special kind of stupid to forget . . .

GRAMS: 'NICE WORK IF YOU CAN GET IT' BY SARAH VAUGHAN. LINK TO–

Scene Five: The Hen and Pewter pub, Saturday night.

F/X: PUB TRIO TUNING UP, AND GENERAL PUB ATMOSPHERE, OVER WHICH–

GEORGE: Well, this is your big night, Roy. Here's to you and the Mrs.

ROY: Cheers, Georgie-Boy. Bottoms up.

GEORGE: I must say you're looking very dapper . . . Lucky I reminded you that it was your wedding anniversary, eh?

ROY: I would have remembered eventually. I knew it was sometime this year . . . Did you get the tickets for me, like I asked?

GEORGE: I did. Here they are.

ROY: Nice work, George. How much do I owe you?

GEORGE: Just consider it my anniversary present to you both.

ROY: Thank you George. I shall definitely remember you in my will for this . . . I won't leave you any money, but I'll definitely say that I remembered you.

GEORGE: Should be a lovely evening.

ROY: Oh, I can guarantee you of that, fella. Tony Bennett's gonna belt out some classics, we're gonna slip on the old feed bag, and then trip the light fandangle 'til dawn . . . or until me bunions start to throb. Whichever comes first.

GEORGE: What time are you leaving?

ROY: Oh, in a couple of hours. I left her ladyship at home, sprucing herself up. She cleans up quite nicely.

GEORGE: She's a very handsome woman, your wife, Roy, if you don't mind me saying . . . ?

ROY: I agree with you, we make a good couple. Drink up, next one's on me.

GEORGE: Cor, this really is a special occasion. It's not only a Ruby wedding anniversary that happens every 40 years, then . . . ?

ROY: George, you're as funny as an operation on my prostate, but just this once I'll let that remark pass. (*Pause*) Hold on a minute, the seat numbers on these tickets aren't together.

GEORGE: Oh, I meant to mention to you about that. I couldn't get two tickets in the same row.

ROY: Are you sure these are in the same theatre?

GEORGE: No, it's alright. Look, this seat is bang in the centre, with a lovely view of the stage. And this seat–

ROY: –is so far away, the ushers have to take you there by husky.

GEORGE: Sorry, Roy. It's all they had left. It was these seats or none at all. I didn't want you and Vi to miss out.

ROY: No, you're right. You did the right thing. This is a big night for Vi and me. I know she would've liked us to sit together, but I'll just have to describe what he looked like to her, afterwards, that's all . . .

GEORGE: I was sort of thinking that you might give *her* the better seat . . .

ROY: What? But . . . it's *Tony Bennett*, man! (*Pause*) Oh . . . alright, but she better get me some peanut raisins in the interval, that's all I'm saying . . .

GEORGE: That seems reasonable.

ROY: I'm a reasonable man.

F/X: PUB GUITARIST PLAYS JARRING CHORD.

ROY: What the hell was that? Barry! Barry, come here a minute!

BARRY: (*Approaching*) What can I do for you gents, same again?

ROY: Barry, what kind of pub is this you're running?

BARRY: How'd you mean, Roy?

ROY: All this noise, man. People come here to damage their liver, not their ear drums.

BARRY: Oh, that's just my boy, Darwin, and a couple of his mates from college. They asked me if their band could play here tonight. Sort of trial basis.

ROY: Well, when are they gonna finish tuning up and actually play?

BARRY: Er . . . They're already doing their fourth song now.

ROY: This is ridiculous, man. You wanna get yourself some proper music in here. You're gonna lose the carriage trade if you keep this mob on stage, fella.

BARRY: I know, but what can I do? He wants to go professional.

ROY: Professional what?

BARRY: He's been practising for ages. That guitar cost me £350.

ROY: So? Dog might have a collar, don't make him a priest!

BARRY: Like I said, what can I do? He's family. (*Exiting*) Yes, Guv, what can I do for you?

ROY: Shocking! You hear that George? This bunch call themselves musicians! Look at the state of them! 'The Unwashed-Unplugged.'

GEORGE:	They'll be alright if someone wants to do a musical version of 'The Planet of the Apes'. Although, you know it's funny in a way. I sort of envy them. Their youth. Starting out.
ROY:	Me, you and Rusty could have wiped the floor with this lot, at their age. Actually, Rusty's better than them as he is now! What did Barry say his son's name was?
GEORGE:	Darwin, I think.
ROY:	'Darwin'? Well, George, I think that is what's known as *irony*.
GEORGE:	Still, at least you'll be able to hear some good stuff tonight.
ROY:	True, true. Big things are gonna happen tonight. It's in the air. Same again, Barry. Look out Tony Bennett. Roy Walcott's in town!

GRAMS: 'LET ME OFF UPTOWN' BY ANITA O'DAY AND ROY ELDRIDGE. LINK TO—

Scene Six: Roy and Vi's bedroom.

BERNADETTE: Oh, Mum, you look lovely.

VI: Oh, this old thing. Just something I dug out of mothballs.

BERNADETTE: Not according to this price tag on the back.

VI: Oh, cut that off for me will you, please?

BERNADETTE: Sure. There you are.

VI: Thanks. I saw this dress in the shop window, and it just sort of spoke to me, y' know.

BERNADETTE: Well it looks very nice on you. What did Dad think of it?

VI: He hasn't seen it yet.

BERNADETTE: Do you think he'll notice that it's new?

VI: Can you see my naked breasts exposed through the material, and a large gaping hole where the bottom should be?

BERNADETTE: Of course not.

VI: Then, no!

BERNADETTE: Well, I hope Dad's made the effort as well.

VI: Actually, your father looks very nice. He's wearing a blue suit.

BERNADETTE: New?

VI: For your father, yes.

BERNADETTE: This side of the Millennium?

VI: Not even this side of the Apollo moon landing . . . but he's given it a brush.

BERNADETTE: And how are you getting there? Ox cart?

VI: Have a little faith in your father for a change, girl. He's going all out tonight.

GRAMS: 'AIN'T MISBEHAVING' BY SARAH VAUGHAN. LINK TO–

Scene Seven: The Hen and Pewter.

ROY: (*Slightly drunk*) So, Barry, it's all arranged. You've made the right decision, fella. Georgie and me will supply the musicians, you supply the venue and all we can drink, and I guarantee you, once word gets round that Roy T-Bone Walcott is back and swingin', you'll have to turn people away from the doors.

BARRY: Well . . . I don't know Roy. No disrespect, but I've never heard you play. I mean, you were a little bit before my time.

ROY: Don't apologise for your lack of musical education, Barry, just use this opportunity to make up for it. I mean, bloody hell, if you're gonna allow Darwin and his tone deaf knuckle draggers to play, you should be begging me to blow some tune. Am I right, George?

GEORGE: You're right, Roy.

ROY:	We're professionals, Barry. Pro's! We've played with some of the greats, man. George here once played with Ella Fitzgerald, herself.
BARRY:	Well . . . Alright, then. Next Sunday. Trial basis only, mind. We'll see how it goes.
ROY:	You're a wise man, Barry. Let's have another drink to seal the bargain.
BARRY:	Alright, same again?
ROY:	Ta.
GEORGE:	Here, Roy, you know I never played with Ella Fitzgerald.
ROY:	I meant to say Bobby Davro, but it doesn't matter. The main thing is, we're back!
GEORGE:	Yeh, but what are we gonna do? At least, if Rusty were still alive, we could have made up a trio, but there's only the two of us.
ROY:	You're right, Georgie. You're right. First thing we need to do is get ourselves a singer.
GEORGE:	A singer?
ROY:	Yep, a girl singer. Add a bit of glamour and sex appeal . . . present company excepted. Give me a bit of paper, I want to make a list. Yeh, a young chick with an angelic set of pipes, and a devilish pair of jugs!
GEORGE:	Well, I don't know Roy.
ROY:	What, worried you might not be able to keep your hands slipping off the keys, cos of all the drooling?
GEORGE:	No, I was thinking more about you. What's Vi gonna say?
ROY:	Well, it's a thought, but I don't think she'd want the job.
GEORGE:	I mean, what's she gonna say now? Isn't she waiting for you . . . ? Tony Bennett . . . ?

ROY: Stop worrying, George. There's plenty of time. Anyway, this is just the sort of news that will put her in a good mood. You know she only wants me to be happy, and when she hears that I'm gonna be making music again . . . Well, she's gonna be hysterical with happiness!

GRAMS: 'WEAK FOR THE MAN' BY DAKOTA STATON. LINK TO–

Scene Eight: Roy and Vi's house.

VI: (*Angry*) I'm gonna kill that man!

BERNADETTE: Alright, Mum. Calm down. Maybe he's had an accident.

VI: Let's hope so.

BERNADETTE: Do you want me to go and look for him?

VI: Why? He's not lost! I know exactly where he is. Drunk at The Hen and Pewter, probably lying face down in his own opinions!

BERNADETTE: Mum, what are you doing?

VI: What does it look like I'm doing? I'm getting undressed. There's no point in wearing a new dress just to stay in and watch telly.

BERNADETTE: Oh, Mum.

VI: I'm fine, Bernadette. You go home. I'm sure Victor and the kids must be wondering what happened to you. There's no point in your evening being ruined as well.

BERNADETTE: Don't do this Mum. You can still go.

VI: How? Your fool of a father has got the tickets! That's assuming there were ever really any tickets in the first place. Besides, I can't go by myself. This is meant to be a wedding anniversary, not a pub widow's jamboree.

BERNADETTE: Of course you can go by yourself. You don't need Dad to have a good time. I'll drive you down to the theatre, maybe we can still buy a ticket at the box office, or perhaps someone's there with an extra one for someone who hasn't turned up.

VI: (*Sudden realisation*) You're right. There might be someone there, who bought two tickets, only to have one of them turned down.

BERNADETTE: Pardon?

VI: Nothing. Just wishful thinking.

BERNADETTE: Shall I take you, then?

VI: (*After a pause*) Yes, why not? This is the last time your father is going to spoil my fun.

BERNADETTE: There you go. If Dad's got enough sense, he'll come down to the theatre to look for you. If not, then it will just be the two of you.

VI: What do you mean?

BERNADETTE: You and . . . Tony Bennett, of course.

VI: Oh . . . Of course.

GRAMS: 'UNTIL I MET YOU' BY TONY BENNETT. LINK TO–

Scene Nine: The theatre.

F/X: GENERAL THEATRE AUDITORIUM PRE-SHOW ATMOSPHERE.

VI: (*Making way to seat along row*) Sorry . . . Excuse me . . . Can I just get past? . . . I beg your pardon . . . Would you mind moving your coat, I think that's my seat.

WOMAN: Oh, I'm sorry. I thought this seat was empty.

ALASTAIR: (*Approaching*) It is.

VI: Alastair!

ALASTAIR: Our seats are over here, Violet. Have you forgotten?

VI: What . . . ?

ALASTAIR:	Excuse us.
WOMAN:	Of course.
VI:	Alastair, what are you doing?
ALASTAIR:	I saw you come in by yourself. Where's your husband?
VI:	Oh, he's . . . he's . . .
ALASTAIR:	He's not here?
VI:	No.
ALASTAIR:	May I ask why?
VI:	I . . . suppose he found something better to do.
ALASTAIR:	Oh, Violet. I'm dreadfully sorry. Forgive me for saying so, but the man is a fool!
VI:	Yesterday I might have argued the point, but today we're of a mind.
ALASTAIR:	To stand a lady up on your wedding anniversary! It's inconceivable!
VI:	My daughter said I don't need him to enjoy myself, so here I am.
ALASTAIR:	And she's absolutely right. She obviously gets her intellect from her mother. And if she also possesses her mother's beauty, then her husband is a very lucky man indeed.
VI:	She does. And he is. Thank you.
ALASTAIR:	Violet, as we are two, responsible adults, on our own for the evening, would you do me the very great honour of being my guest?
VI:	Well, I don't know. It's one thing to be spending my anniversary on my own, but it's quite another to be spending it with another man.
ALASTAIR:	I see what you mean . . . But don't think of it as spending your anniversary with me, think of it as spending your anniversary with Tony Bennett.
VI:	Well . . . if you put it that way (*Sings*) 'I left my heart in San Francisco . . .'

83

GRAMS: 'LET'S FACE THE MUSIC AND DANCE' BY TONY BENNETT. LINK TO–

Scene Ten: Roy's house. Midnight.

F/X: CLOCK STRIKING MIDNIGHT. KEYS JINGLING IN A LOCK. DOOR CREAKING OPEN.

ROY: (*Whispering, very drunk*) Vi . . . ? Vi . . . ? It's me, darlin'. I'm back now. Where are you? I know I'm a little, teensy weensy bit late . . . but it's alright . . . I bought chips, so you don't have to cook. I got your favourite, sweetheart, haddock. I asked them to do your chips without vinegar, cos I know you don't like it . . . But I don't think they heard me, so yours might not taste so wonderful, but still . . . I was the last customer, so at least it's a nice big portion. I've got some wonderful news, Vi. Guess what? Give up? Me and George are putting together a new band. Yeh, I know, it's beautiful! That's why I was late. You see, the landlord at The Hen has asked us to play next Sunday, so we had to make plans, y'see? Vi . . . ? Vi . . . ? Vi-sey-Wi-sey? Are you hiding, you little saucepot? Where are you?

F/X: KNOCKING ON BEDROOM DOOR.

ROY: Vi, are you in bed? There's a big slab of greasy fish here with your name on it.

F/X: DOOR OPENING. LIGHT BEING SWITCHED ON.

ROY Where is she? Vi . . . ? Vi . . . ?

GRAMS: 'I COULDN'T SLEEP A WINK LAST NIGHT' BY FRANK SINATRA. LINK TO–

Scene Eleven: Bernadette's bedroom.

F/X: PHONE RINGING.

VICTOR: Hello.

ROY: (*Drunk*) Where is she? Put her on the line!

VICTOR: I beg your pardon? Is that you Mr Walcott?

ROY: Of course. Who else could it be? Who is that?

VICTOR: It's me, Victor.

ROY: Who?

VICTOR: Victor. (*Pause*) Your son-in-law . . . ?

ROY: I see . . . What are you doing there?

VICTOR: Er . . . This is my house. I live here.

ROY: Does my daughter know?

VICTOR: Er . . . Yes. We've been together for 17 years. We have two children.

ROY: How dare you?

VICTOR: Sorry . . . ?

ROY: I'm a married man! You can't talk to me like that, fella. Put Bernadette on the line, and count yourself lucky.

VICTOR: (*Calling*) 'B', your Dad's on the phone.

BERNADETTE: Does he sound upset?

VICTOR: Er . . . Yeh, as in the expression: 'Upset as a newt'!

BERNADETTE: Dad. Aren't you ashamed of yourself?

ROY: What?

BERNADETTE: Mum waited ages for you. How could you just not turn up?

ROY: Listen to me, girl. What takes place between your mother and me, is our own business, and nothing to do with you!

BERNADETTE: I see . . . What do you want?

ROY: You don't know where she is do you? I've looked all over the house, and she's not here.

BERNADETTE: Have you checked under the doormat? Isn't that where you usually expect to find her?

ROY: What?

BERNADETTE: You just don't get it do you? You think you can just ride roughshod over her feelings, and everything will be okay.

ROY: No, you've lost me . . .

BERNADETTE: Mum's gone out Dad. Gone to the concert! Gone to dinner! Gone dancing! Ring any bells?

ROY: Look, something great happened tonight . . . and I will explain the situation to your mother, not you. I know she's there, and I want to speak to her now!

BERNADETTE: Well, don't hold your breath . . . actually, no, do! You know, you're right Dad, something great did happen tonight. Mum finally took a step away from you.

ROY: Listen, stop talking in riddles, and put her on . . .

BERNADETTE: She's not here! She called me earlier on to say that she is having the time of her life . . . Which I can well believe, because, guess what . . . ? You're not with her.

ROY: Look, I am the parent, you are the child. Have some manners.

BERNADETTE: Sleep it off, Dad. I'm hanging up now, before I say something that I might regret.

ROY: No, that was your husband, when he said 'I do'. You good for nothing little–

F/X: DISCONNECTED TONE.

VI: What did he say?

BERNADETTE: You mean in between the 80% proof insults . . . ? I think he only half-believed me when I told him you weren't here.

VI: Oh, Lord! That means he'll come round here. I don't want to see him. I don't!

BERNADETTE: I think he's probably too far gone to try and make the trip here tonight. Let him stew, and decide what to do in the morning.

VI: What do you mean?

BERNADETTE: Well . . . Where you're going to live and things. You're welcome to stay here for as long as you want to, of course, but I just thought that you'd want to make a start on getting your own place.

VI: Hold on, child. You're going a bit too fast for me.

BERNADETTE: Well, you've left him haven't you?

VI: Well . . . In the sense that I'm not in the house with him – yes.

BERNADETTE: And don't you feel an almost overwhelming sense of relief and liberation? You said yourself that once you stopped thinking about Dad this evening, you enjoyed yourself more than you have done in years.

VI: Yes, that's true, but–

BERNADETTE: Well, just think of this evening as the beginning of the rest of your life.

VI: I . . . I'm going to bed. Goodnight.

BERNADETTE: (*Smug*) Goodnight. You know it makes sense.

VICTOR: Goodnight, Violet.

F/X: DOOR CLOSING.

VICTOR: What are you doing?

BERNADETTE: What?

VICTOR: My God, you've become the anti-Cupid! You're actually trying to split your parents up?

BERNADETTE: Mum doesn't know what's best for her at the moment. I'm just trying to help. Sometimes you have to be harsh about it, that's all.

VICTOR: And, remind me, they rejected your application for landmine victim support worker because . . . ?

BERNADETTE: Shut up and kiss me.

VICTOR: But your Mum's in the next room.

87

BERNADETTE: Victor, we've got two kids. I think even my Mother may have guessed that we've had sex by now.

VICTOR: Yeh, but aren't you worried about the noise?

BERNADETTE: No. I'm sure she'll just sit in there quietly. (*Seductively*) Now come here . . .

VICTOR/BERNADETTE: (*Muffled moans of pleasure*)

GRAMS: 'IT'S ALRIGHT WITH ME' BY JESSE BELVIN. LINK TO–

Scene Twelve: Bernadette and Victor's garden. 25 minutes later.

F/X: 2 PAIRS OF FEET TRAMPING UP A GRAVEL PATH.

GEORGE: Are you sure this is such a good idea, Roy? I mean, she must be pretty upset.

ROY: That's exactly why we're here. Now, throw a pebble up to the window, Georgie.

GEORGE: Right-o.

F/X: GENTLE TAP OF PEBBLE ON WINDOW PANE.

ROY: Anything?

GEORGE: Nothing yet.

ROY: Try it again. Put a bit of a spin on it.

F/X: GENTLE TAP ON WINDOW PANE.

ROY: Any sign of her?

GEORGE: No. Are you sure she's here? Didn't Bernadette say she was out?

ROY: That was just a load of old flannel, Georgie, just flannel. I know she's in there somewhere, and I intend to get her out! Here, let me have a go.

F/X: LOUD SMASH OF GLASS.

GEORGE: Er . . . Yes, I think that did the trick.

F/X: WINDOW BEING OPENED.

VIOLET:	What the – George?
GEORGE:	Er . . . Good evening Violet. Roy, your husband, has something he would like to say to you.
ROY:	Nice one George. Alright, hit it!

F/X: 'PLAY' BUTTON BEING PRESSED ON TAPE RECORDER.

GRAMS: CRACKLY BACKING TRACK TO 'THEY CAN'T TAKE THAT AWAY FROM ME'.

MUTED TROMBONE SOLO, OVER WHICH–

F/X: WINDOW BEING OPENED.

BERNADETTE: Oh my God.

VICTOR: What's going on?

BERNADETTE: It's Dad. He's . . . serenading Mum with her favourite song.

VICTOR: He sounds pretty good.

BERNADETTE: (*Defeated*) Yes . . . I know.

ROY: Alright, George, easy on the maracas. (*Sings*) 'The way you wear your hat, the way you sip your tea. The memory of all that. Oh, no they can't take that away from me – No –'

LAST PHRASE PLAYED ON TROMBONE.

ROY: Vi, are you coming home, or do I have to come in and get you?

VI: Give me a minute.

F/X: KNOCK ON BEDROOM DOOR.

VICTOR: Come in, Violet.

F/X: DOOR OPENING.

VI: I suppose you heard all of that?

VICTOR: Us, and our local MP by morning, I should expect.

VI: I think I should go home and talk things over with your father.

VICTOR: Alright, Violet. If you think it's for the best.

VI: I do. (*Pause*) Bernadette . . . ?

BERNADETTE: (*Sadly*) Alright, Mum.

VI: I'll give you a call tomorrow.

F/X: DOOR CLOSING.

VICTOR: Are you okay?

BERNADETTE: Hey, she's a grown woman. Just goes to show there's no age limit on stupid mistakes.

VICTOR: Or pouting when you don't get your own way . . . ?

BERNADETTE: Yeh . . . Well . . .

VICTOR: (*Fondly*) Come here. Cheer up, I promise we'll get you some Dalmatian puppies to drown in the morning. (*Pause*) Ow!

GRAMS: 'RIGHT NOW' BY MEL TORME. LINK TO–

Scene Thirteen: Vi and Roy's House. The following day.

F/X: TELEPHONE RINGING.

VI: Hello . . . Oh, hello Bernadette. Are we speaking now? . . . Good. I'm glad you understand . . . Oh, y'know . . . You can't expect change overnight . . . No, he's not here right now . . . As a matter of fact, I'm just off to see him . . . Yes, that's right . . . Oh, by the way, your father asked me to pass on a message . . . He says, do you think you could get the Police to drop the attempted burglary charges against him and George, as they've got a gig on Sunday . . . Well, at least think about it . . . Bernadette . . . ? Bernadette . . . ?

END THEME MUSIC AND ANNOUNCEMENTS.

6. Drafts and Rewrites

There are probably few greater feelings for a writer than finishing a script. Yes, hearing that script read aloud by good actors for the first time is a thrill, and of course, seeing or hearing the broadcast version takes some beating (and we shall be looking at both these events in a later chapter), but knowing that you've started out with a blank sheet of paper, and filled it with your ideas, gives a great sense of achievement, and is not to be undervalued. However, don't be tempted to think that your job is over as regards that particular script. This could not be further from the truth.

You know your characters, you can hear how they speak, you know the way they feel about one another, and you're comfortable with their surroundings. You've structured a watertight plot and subplot, and come to a satisfactory resolution. You've wrung every last ounce of humour out of the situation, your characters have said all they wish to say on the matter, and you've placed your final full stop. As far as you (or you and your writing partner) are concerned, your script is *finished*.

Well . . . it's probably only 'finished' if you intend to lock your script away in a drawer somewhere, and never show it to an actual radio or TV producer. The reality of the situation is that, even though you may think your script is complete and ready for the world, once a broadcaster or production company becomes involved, you'll quickly realise that you've only taken your first steps towards a final draft. A producer will generally have been in the business quite a bit longer than the first time writer (unless it's your 'luck' to team up with someone who was working in the canteen the day before you came along), and as such, he or she will have one or two ideas regarding your scripted efforts (although, of course, experienced writers are by

91

no means immune to the whims of producers either). You will probably find that your perfectly formed, hilariously written script has been picked apart, restructured, tinkered with, and just plain changed before you leave the office after an initial meeting. As frustrating as this will undoubtedly be (and believe us – we've been there many, many times) you just have to learn to accept this as part of the process. If you are the kind of writer who disregards any form of outside input, then the likelihood of a long lasting career in TV or radio is pretty slim at best. The creation of a sitcom is a collaborative effort, and not just between yourself and your writing partner. The producer's suggestions may be perfectly valid, and, of course, any opportunity to improve your work should be embraced, which isn't to suggest that you blindly go along with every new idea, but rather, remain objective. If your reasons for a particular line of dialogue or plot twist are sound, and you can justify your use of them, then only the most overbearing of producers will insist that they be changed.

However, bear in mind that producers, script editors etc, are all fallible human beings, (although, if you are on the receiving end of the drastic edit, you may be inclined to think this way anyway) and occasionally they may just be *wrong* about something. It happens, whether we like it or not, but your job as a writer is to simply go back to the keyboard, and try to implement those changes. Yes, of course we make it sound easy, and No, it probably won't be, but Yes it has to be done!

Once your script is in the hands of a producer, you no longer fully dictate the shape of your story or characters. Of course, you will have your say as regards the direction in which a particular script may be going, and as we stated, this is a collaborative effort, so of course you won't suddenly find yourself relegated to fetching the tea while strangers rake over your work, but you also have to accept that the script is no longer 'your baby', and be prepared to share the creation of it with others.

If it sounds like we're trying to hammer this point home – then good! We are! It may seem unfair, or a liberty to have someone who was not sitting alongside you as you slaved over the first draft, telling you to go away and 'make it funnier' etc, but that is the nature of the business. Take heart, all the great sitcom writers went through exactly this same process, writing, rewriting, cutting, amending, until they came up with the finished versions of episodes that we now know and love. True, it's unlikely that Galton and Simpson or John Sullivan were 'dictated to' as much once they had a proven success on their hands, but you can rest assured that they suffered the same frustrations that you will when they started out. However, who's to say whether or not we would have found the first draft of 'The Blood Donor' funnier than the one we actually saw. Nobody knows! The point is, the script went through the collaborative process and came out as the classic we know and love.

Having your script finally commissioned is, of course, a wonderful feeling, knowing that all those rewrites have finally paid off, and your series, or at the very least a pilot will be made. However, this may not be the end of your rewriting.

Once a series is commissioned, then other members of the team will be suddenly brought on board. If you have been dealing solely with the executive producer up to now, you may suddenly find that a brand new producer has been appointed, not to mention a script editor, and both of them will have their own ideas as to the content of your script. True, your script has been given the green light, and the powers that be are finally satisfied with your 'final' version – but once others come on board, then you have a whole new set of collaborators to work with, and you may find yourself having to rewrite the whole thing again.

With that in mind, let's take a look at the main individual who should be battling on your side, but who you may, on occasion, find yourself battling with:

The script editor

The script editor will usually be someone who has worked with the production company or the particular network before, and who therefore knows the various requirements, sometimes creative, but often technical, that your employers will have for the finished script.

It's the script editor's job to act as a go-between for you and the other people on the production. You will find that if you have a friend or colleague who already acts as your script editor, there will usually be a great deal of resistance to using them on the production after it gets commissioned. Production companies much prefer to have someone who is 'in their camp', as getting you to deliver the script on time is also part of the script editor's job. *A word of caution here*: as a first time writer you are unlikely to have the clout to impose your own script editor on the production, no matter how much work they have put in before the commission, so be very careful about promising anything in advance to someone like this. In fact avoid promising ANYONE rewards based on your getting a commission – many friendships have broken up when these promises couldn't be delivered.

As we've already noted, the relationship between writer and script editor is an interesting one. Technically the script editor is there to help you write a better script, as well as make sure it conforms to whatever guidelines the producer and network dictate.

A good script editor will try hard to get an idea of the script you are trying to write, and try to bring the best possible version of *that script* out of you. They will identify problems and pick up on things you may miss in the script, but always with a view to helping you solve the problem. Yes, they may cut out some of your favourite things because of time constraints, but *usually* (when the pain has dulled) you will admit that the script is better and moves faster.

Unfortunately, you need to be aware that as comedy isn't as large an industry in the UK as it is in the USA, you may also get the *other* kind of script editor: you've heard the phrase 'Those who can't, teach?' – well, guess what some of those who can't write do? An inexperienced script editor will communicate the changes they *think* the producer wants, only to find that when you make those changes, the producer wanted something completely different. Be wary also of the 'script editor' who is primarily a writer themselves . . . instead of helping you write the script that's inside you, they will invariably give you notes based on the script they would write if they were in your place.

As we stated earlier, your key strategy in this scenario is not to lose your cool, no matter how much you are tempted. Remember that the producer is the one who employed the script editor, so by bad mouthing the person in the job, you are also putting down the producer's judgement. Even if you are questioning the script editor's comments, do so with extreme courtesy – getting a reputation for being difficult won't help your career prospects. Now, while we're not suggesting that you become a complete doormat (we'd be lying if we said that we haven't had the occasional 'heated difference of opinion' with script editors from time to time), we do recommend that you listen to all ideas courteously – and pick your battles carefully. Try to ensure though, that if someone points out a problem, they are prepared to come up with a solution to the problem too. You don't have to use their suggestion, of course – but it's a very good way of dissuading people from demanding changes just because they can. (Good producers and script editors will usually suggest solutions to problems they raise as a matter of course.)

Request that all comments and requests for changes are given to you on paper or preferably by email, and if at all possible, copy the producer in on all your correspondence. That way you'll find out pretty quickly if you are getting the information direct from the person who pays your wages or through an unreliable filter.

Lest we sound paranoid, we should point out that it is also possible to get a script editor who is also a seasoned sitcom writer themselves, or who has worked on top quality sitcoms, in which case their advice and experience can be invaluable not just for the show you are working on, but also for your own learning and development as a writer.

Of course, you may relish the prospect of someone giving you the benefit of their experience, and be more than happy to completely alter your script accordingly. If this is you, then you have a very healthy outlook on life – and can you tell us your secret (not to mention the name of your chemist). As for all other writers, we just have to bite the bullet, making sense of changes we have been asked to implement, cutting lines of dialogue that we think are perfectly sound, or losing whole scenes and characters in draft six that you were asked to include in draft three and couldn't see the reason for putting in there in the first place (yes, this has happened to us!) It's part of the job – end of story!

The sitcom (re)writer

Whoever coined the phrase 'Writing is Rewriting' must have worked on quite a few sitcoms, because that adage applies in spades to this kind of writing. Anything from four to twenty rewrites isn't unusual before the script gets off the writer's computer and into the production stage. You can't really blame the producer – after all they're going to invest a lot of money in the show, so they can be forgiven for wanting to make the script 'perfect' before they start paying through the nose for actors' fees and booking expensive studio time.

Remember though to keep every new version of the script from draft to finished version as a separate file on your computer. Frequently, new suggestions don't prove to be as funny as the original material, which then has to be reinstated in yet another draft (and when you write your 'how to' book on sitcoms you'll find the different scripts very useful to illustrate the points you're making!) In particular, one phenomenon, which affects comedy in a way that drama avoids, is the fact that *most jokes are only funny the first time you hear them*.

It's very important to keep confidence in jokes that you know work, so that you can also maintain that confidence in others – otherwise a perfectly good line may be altered or dropped as 'familiarity breeds contempt', and then replaced by something, which is actually less funny, but just seems fresher because of novelty value.

As an example of just how much your script can change from first draft to final 'collaborative' version, we have included an extract from *Stage Fright*, a children's series we created a few years ago. The basic premise of the series is that Sam, a 14 year-old girl, attends a stage school, and discovers that the school is built on the site of an old nightclub that was bombed during WW2. Little known American big band diva Dolores Jones was the only person killed during the blast, whilst on a UK tour, and because of a celestial administrative mix-up, is forced to haunt the school. Although she has a dislike of kids, she finds herself drawn to Sam, the only living person who can see her, effectively becoming her 'guardian angel'. There's a little more to it than that, but you get the gist.

The extract comes from an episode that would occur somewhere in the middle of a series. As we mentioned in Chapter 4, producers generally ask for a sample script that will show how the characters interact once a series is established, as opposed to the pilot episode, which is more about setting everything up.

Stage Fright – sample script

Episode: *Please Don't Talk About Me When I'm Gone.*

By John Byrne & Marcus Powell

Scene One: 'SWITCHED-ON TV' STUDIO.
Close up on TV screen. On screen are Jamie and Sada, the two young presenters of 'SWITCHED-ON TV', a popular cable TV entertainment show.

JAMIE:	. . . Wow, that was absolutely wicked! There'll be more cartoon craziness from Groovy Grizelda, The Disco Witch next week. . . Laugh . . . ? I nearly went out and bought a Gary Barlow CD.
SADA:	Personally, I like Pop-Cat the best. I think Grizelda's really horrible to him. I bet he gets his own back one day . . . But you'll have to keep watching us here on SWITCHED-ON TV to find out.
JAMIE:	True, but that's all from us this week. Don't forget on next week's show we're gonna have more celebrity victims in the Gungey Goldfish Bowl–
SADA:	–All the latest 'Poptastic' goss–
JAMIE:	–And more movie and TV news than your Grandad's got hairs up his nose.
SADA:	Oo-er! And don't miss our exclusive interview and live performance from the abso-bloomin'-lutely Megapopalicious Bug Daddy B. I just love his songs.
JAMIE:	You're right there, Sada. Bug Daddy B is funkier than the entire Funky family from

upper Funkton on the Wold, in East Funkingshire . . . And that's pretty funky.

SADA: (*Laughing, insincerely*) Oh, Jamie, you're so funny.

JAMIe: . . . Funnier than the funny fraternity from F–? (*Sada places her hand over his mouth*)

SADA: –Say Goodbye, Jamie.

JAMIE: (*Muffled by Sada's hand*) Mmm-mmm.

SADA: We're outta here! I'm off skiing, and I think Jamie's got to tidy his room, but we're gonna leave you with a sneak preview of Bug Daddy B's latest video: 'Suburban Ghetto Smackdown Jam.' See ya next Friday, guys.

Scene Two: BUG DADDY B'S VIDEO.
Video appears on screen, featuring Bug Daddy B dressed in Gangsta rapper outfit i.e., long white coat, suit and hat to match, dark glasses and a gold-topped cane, flanked by half-a-dozen female dancers.

B D B: (*Rapping*) . . . I tried to ride in my car, but I didn't get far.

You know my style's been cramped, because my wheel's got clamped.

I jumped upon the bus and tried to pay half fare, but the conductor grabbed me by my underwear.

He said: 'How old are you?', I said 'I'm just thirteen.'

He said: 'You're big for your age,' I said 'I eat all my greens.'

I said: 'D'You know who I am? My name is Bug Daddy B.'

He said: 'Wow, I've just been playing your new CD.'

So he let me go, apologised for the fuss.

I gave him my autograph – Guess what? He gave *me* the bus!

1940s swing band style sample and scat vocal chorus begin to play, and we see the silhouette of a woman singing at a microphone.

Scene Three: STAGE SCHOOL CANTEEN.
Sam and Jools in the Stacey Parrish Academy for Performing Arts canteen, sitting at a table, watching the programme on TV.

JOOLS: (*Dancing and humming along to the chorus in her chair*) Aha . . . hmm hmm . . . Yeh . . . Baby . . . Skiddly diddly be bop shu bam . . . etc.

Jools, sporting an elaborate new hairstyle, is becoming increasingly animated, eventually swinging her arms out and knocking a bowl of soup out of the hands of a boy passing their table. She carries on swaying, oblivious to the accident she has caused. The boy looks at Sam. Sam shrugs an apology.

SAM: (*To the boy*) . . . Sorry . . . I'm thinking of trading her in for a gerbil. They're so much easier to housetrain . . .

The boy shakes his head in resignation, and exits the way he entered.

SAM: (*To Jools*) Ooh, Ooh! Hello . . . is everything all right up there on Planet Jools?

JOOLS: Oh, don't you just love him . . . ?

SAM: Who . . . ? (*She looks up at screen*) You mean Big Baby Bean?

JOOLS: (*Mock indignant*) How dare you?!? It's *Bug Daddy B.*

SAM: I think mine sounded better.

JOOLS: What?!?

SAM: Alright, I'm sorry. 'Bug Daddy B'.

JOOLS: That's better . . . And smile when you say that next time. (*She continues humming and dancing, but more subdued than before*) I love this song.

SAM: Honestly Jools, I don't know how you can like his stuff. This song drives me crazy. Everywhere I go, I keep hearing it.

JOOLS: That's because it's the lick!

SAM: I think I even heard my Dad whistling it the other night, but the tune turned into the music from *Eastenders*. Mind you, everything my Dad whistles turns into the music from *Eastenders*.

JOOLS: Well that just goes to show that Bug Daddy B appeals to all age groups, from teenagers to – what age is your dad?

SAM: 38

JOOLS: – to *really old* people.

SAM: (*Does BDB impression*) 'I tried to ride in my car, blah blah blah. My CD's lousy, but I'm still a star.'

JOOLS: Ha Ha Ha. What do you know about music? You're still waiting for Bob the Builder to tour. (*Jools smiles at Sam*) 'Can- he- fix- it?'

SAM: 'Yes- he- can!'

They both laugh.

JOOLS: (*Excited*) Oh, Sam, I still can't believe we're gonna be doing our work experience on the same show, in the same week as Bug Daddy B.

SAM: Ah, is that why you've got yourself all done up?

JOOLS: You know it, girl. I can't meet my fave rapper without getting a new 'coif'. Do you like the colour?

SAM: (*Indicating Jools' hairstyle*) Exactly what colour is that, Jools?

JOOLS: The hairdresser said it was 'a cool fusion of Midnight Cerise blending a subtle dash of Puce'.

SAM: Oh, I see. (*Pause*) 'Black with a bit of red'. (*Pause*) Nice. It's really lucky that Miss Parrish's brother is the producer, and he's

letting us all work on the show. Even if it means
that I have to keep hearing that song, just think,
we get to work with Sada and *Jamie*. (*They
both sigh*)

JOOLS: I know, it's too wicked for words! 'SWITCHED-
ON TV'. Can I get a 'Whoo-Hoo' . . . ?

*Sam and Jools both leap to their feet and do a simultaneous
Cheerleader-type movement, ending in a jubilant cry of
'Whoo–Hoo, Honey Bunny! Boom Chaka Boom!' As they
do a final cheer, Jools swings her arms out, just as the boy
walks past carrying another bowl of soup. The soup goes all
over him again, but this time both Sam and Jools fail to
notice. The boy hangs his head in silence and turns to exit.*

JOOLS: I've been watching this show for years, and
now I'm gonna be on it.

SAM: No, Jools. We're not gonna be *on it*. We're
gonna be running around, doing odd jobs
behind the scenes for a week.

JOOLS: Yeh, but you never know, they might be on the
look out for a talented young Asian girl with
oodles of pizzazz, and an eye-catching new
hairstyle, to present an item on fashion or
something . . .

SAM: Get her! A splodge of gel and she thinks she's
become Davina McCall.

*Jools' mobile phone begins to ring on the table. Jools makes
no attempt to answer it, but sits, smiling enigmatically at
Sam.*

SAM: Jools, aren't you gonna get that?

JOOLS: Not yet. I want all the music to play first.
Listen.

*As Sam listens carefully to the ring tone her face falls. The
melody is exactly the same as the Bug Daddy B song.*

SAM: Oh no. Not Bug Daddy B's song . . . again! Did
you have to . . . ?

JOOLS: You love it really . . . You just don't know it yet.

Jools moves to the tune while smirking at Sam.

SAM: (*Getting annoyed*) You know, Jools, you're right. I do love it! Let me show you how much –

Sam lunges for the phone. Jools quickly grabs the phone, and, laughing, answers it.

JOOLS: (*Into phone*) Hello (*To Sam*) It's Fitz. (*Into phone*) Alright Fitz, where are you? What . . .? I can't make you out . . . No, you're breaking up . . . Listen, Sam and I are in the canteen. Come and find us . . . (*She hangs up*) He's a funny fish, that boy.

SAM: Why, what's he up to?

JOOLS: Don't know. Couldn't make him out. Something about 'how much did your cat cost you?' or something like that.

SAM: Why does he want to know how much you paid for your cat?

JOOLS: I don't know, that's none of his business! (*Pause*) Hold on, I haven't *got* a cat!

Fitz approaches the table, dressed in giant cat outfit. He stands behind Jools, who fails to see him. He waves to Sam.

SAM: (*Looking directly at Fitz*) Jools, do you think he might have said 'I'm- in- a- cat- costume' . . . ?

JOOLS: (*Still unaware of Fitz behind her*) No . . . I don't think so. No, that would be silly. Why would he say a thing like that?

Fitz places a giant paw on Jools' shoulder. Jools leaps out of her seat and strikes a Karate pose.

JOOLS: (*Shocked*) Fitz, that better be you, or I'm about to kick some kitty-butt!

FITZ: (*Removing head*) Hold on it's me . . . Or should I say: It's 'Pop-Cat'.

SAM/JOOLS: What?

FITZ: You know, from the 'Groovy Grizelda, the Disco Witch' cartoon.

SAM: I don't get it . . .

FITZ: Well, Miss Parrish got a call from her brother, the producer at 'SWITCHED-ON TV' yesterday, and he asked her if she had any students who fancied doing something a bit different for their work placement, so she sent me down to meet him.

SAM: And he told you to dress up like Pop-Cat?

FITZ: Yeh, it's great isn't it? He thought that because we are all from a stage school, some of us might like to get the chance to perform on the show in some way.

JOOLS: (*To Sam*) . . . Told you . . .

FITZ: So instead of just having Pop-Cat in the cartoon, they'll have him dancing in the studio as well. I'm gonna get to groove in the background when the bands are on.

SAM: Ooh, nice one Fitzy. So come on then, show us some of your moggy moves.

FITZ: OK. Let me put my head back on, so you get the full effect. (*He does so*) Right, get a load of this fancy paw work . . . (*He does a couple of clumsy dance steps, before eventually falling over*) . . . Or I will as soon as I get used to wearing the suit. It's the tail. It keeps getting in the way . . .

JOOLS: (*Laughing*) What are you talking about, you always dance like that. In fact, not normally *that good*. If you knew how silly you looked . . . I can't believe you're gonna go on telly dressed like that . . . Dancing in front of celebrities, and everything . . . (*She laughs, hysterically*)

Stacey Parrish enters, holding a clipboard.

STACEY: Ah, Jools, there you are. I'm glad you're so happy about it.

JOOLS: Pardon Miss.

STACEY: . . . Well it's not every young girl who would agree to do it, but I know you're a real trouper. That's why I put your name down for it.

JOOLS: I'm sorry Miss Parrish, I don't understand.

STACEY: (*To Fitz*) Oh, didn't you tell her?

FITZ: Not yet Miss.

STACEY: Well allow me. Fitz here is obviously getting into the swing of his role as 'Pop-Cat', but what is 'Pop-Cat' without his 'Disco Witch'? (*She places her hand on Jools' shoulder. Jools smiles, confused*) You, dear, YOU. Have fun.

Stacey turns on her heels and exits.

JOOLS: (*In shock*) Did she just say that I had to . . . ?

SAM: (*Nodding*) . . . She did.

JOOLS: But I'm gonna be dressed as a . . .

SAM: I know . . .

JOOLS: But I've just had my hair done! (*She starts crying*)

The boy with the bowl of soup approaches the table for a third time. He pauses, looks at the giant cat, pauses again, then pours the soup over himself.

BOY: (*To Jools*) There . . . are you happy now . . . ?

Scene Four: SAM'S BEDROOM. EVENING.
Sam's annoying younger brother Marcus furtively enters the room. He looks around to see if he has been seen, and crosses to Sam's chest of drawers. He begins humming Bug Daddy B's tune to himself as he rummages through the things in the drawer. Sam quietly enters the room, holding her cat, and spots him. She places the cat on the floor.

SAM: Marcus! What do you think you're doing? And don't bother telling me that you wandered into the wrong room by mistake again, cos this looks nothing like your kennel.

MARCUS: (*Continuing his search, regardless*) If you must know, I was looking for one of my Whistle Pops.

SAM: Your what? Why would one of your lollipops be in my drawer?

MARCUS: Don't think I don't know that you've always got your eye on my stuff.

SAM: What? *Me* with my eye on *your* . . . ? Listen you little stinkpot . . .

MARCUS: Here it is . . .

He holds up a skirt from the drawer, with his lollipop stuck to it.

SAM: My skirt! What have you done to it?

Marcus pulls the lollipop off the skirt, sucks it, then blows the Bug Daddy B tune.

MARCUS: No, it's still alright. (*He continues to play the tune*)

Sam picks up a pillow from her bed and chases him out of the room.

SAM: Out! Out, before I tell Dad to take you back to the pond where we found you! (*Calling after him*) And don't think he wouldn't gladly swap you for a new pair of trainers if I asked him to, either.

She shuts the door and crosses to the chest of drawers. As she is about to shut the drawer she hears Dolores' voice coming from inside.

DOLORES: Hold on a minute there, Missy.

SAM: Dolores?

DOLORES: No, this is the voice of your underwear. Of course it's me.

She magically floats out of the drawer, stretching to full size and landing in front of Sam.

DOLORES: 'Jeez Louise'! I thought that little brat would never high-tail it out of here.

SAM: Where have you been? I haven't seen you in about a week.

DOLORES: Ten days, six hours and 37 minutes of pure joy, to be exact . . . but who's counting . . . ? Did you miss me, kiddo?

SAM: Not really! Where were you?

DOLORES: Well excuuuuse me! Even we ladies of the ghostly persuasion are allowed a little rest and relaxation from time to time. For your information, oh petulant one, I've been on holiday. The Cloud 12 Hotel and Celestial Spa. It was great. Shakespeare was there. Oh, by the way, he says that if you ever need any help with your English homework, just let him know.

SAM: You met *William Shakespeare?*

DOLORES: Oh, sure. Nice guy. He sure talks funny, but he plays a mean game of Scrabble. Oh, I had a ball. I'm tellin' ya, kid, you ain't had a heavenly holiday 'til you've had a holiday in heaven. It's to die for.

SAM: (*Groaning at bad joke*) Good grief.

DOLORES: Oh lighten up, I've been waiting for an excuse to say that all week. So, what ya been up to while I've been away? Don't tell me, let me guess: Gossiping with Jools, going goo-goo eyed over some boy in a magazine, and popping your zits . . . ? Am I close . . . ?

SAM: For your information, I'm starting my work experience placement tomorrow.

DOLORES: Your what?

SAM: My work experience placement. A company or organisation allows students to come and work for a week, to give them an idea of what it's like to have a job. In my case, tomorrow I start working at the studios of 'SWITCHED-ON TV'.

DOLORES: Hey now! That sounds kinda groovy! I've never been to a TV studio before. I was invited once to do a test broadcast, back in '42, when I was still . . . you know . . . but they chose a balancing dog act to do the show instead, which as I have always said, is their loss, cos if there is one chick who should have been caught on camera, it's most definitely yours truly. So, what time do we start?

106

SAM:	What do you mean 'we?' You're not coming! Please tell me you're not coming . . .
DOLORES:	What do you mean 'I'm not coming . . . ?' You don't think I'm gonna allow my little earthbound munchkin to go along to the big bad TV studio without her auntie Dolores floating along . . .
SAM:	. . . But . . .

She is interrupted by a knock on the door.

SAM:	Come in.

Paul enters.

PAUL:	Hi Sam, here's your lunch money for tomorrow.
SAM:	Thanks Dad.
PAUL:	I suppose you must be pretty excited about going to the studio in the morning.
SAM:	(*To Dolores*) . . . Well, I was . . .
PAUL:	Pardon.
SAM:	Yeh . . . I can't wait. It's gonna be great.
PAUL:	'Great'? I didn't think you all still said 'Great'. Don't you mean it's 'Da Bomb'?
SAM:	(*Laughing*) No, Dad. Where did you get that from? 'Da Bomb' is so 1999.
PAUL:	Well . . . that's what I heard that rapper Big Baggy Boo saying on the radio.
SAM:	Oh, Dad . . . That's 'Bug Da–' . . . Oh, never mind.

Dolores pops up beside Paul and blows on his cheek.

PAUL:	(*Feeling the breeze*) Brrr. Have you got your window open, Sam?
SAM:	Er, no Dad. I think there must be a draught coming from somewhere.

Dolores leaps into the body of the cat sitting on the windowsill. The 'cat' then leaps into the arms of Paul, and begins purring. From Sam's point of view we see Dolores in Paul's arms, smiling contentedly. Sam is completely amazed by the feat.

PAUL: I don't know what's gotten into this cat of yours lately, but all of a sudden we seem to have become the best of friends. (*He places the cat gently on the bed*) Well, dinner will be ready in half an hour, Sam.

SAM: OK Dad. I'm just sorting out what I'm going to wear tomorrow. We young media types have to look our best, you know. I've gotta look heavy while I'm making my way through the corridors of power. Wheeling and dealing with all the top 'prods', and schmoozing with the celebs . . .

PAUL: (*Amused*) . . . I see . . . (*He turns to exit*) Well, if you find a spare moment in between all your high powered meetings, Miss Spielberg . . . it's your turn to do the laundry this week.

SAM: Yes, Dad.

Paul exits. Dolores leaps out of the cat's body and appears next to Sam. The cat lets out a strangulated 'Meeeee-oooowww!' shakes its head, and runs out of the room.

SAM: How did you do that? That was amazing!

DOLORES: Oh, that little thing . . . It's nothing for a girl who was voted Most Promising Poltergeist at last year's annual Ghost and Spectre awards . . . Or 'The Spookies' as we in the haunting biz like to call them.

SAM: But what about poor 'Tibby'? Didn't it hurt?

DOLORES: 'Hurt?' No, here see for yourself.

Dolores leaps into Sam's body and poses in front of the mirror.

SAM: (*As Dolores*) . . . See, honey. It don't hurt a bit! (*Looking in mirror*) How on earth can you wear these clothes?

Dolores leaps back out of Sam's body.

SAM: Yuk! Don't ever do that again!

DOLORES: Trust me, Lamb Chop; it was no picnic for me either. Squeezing *this much* Jazz Diva into *that much* Juvenile Delinquent isn't my idea of a swingin' night out. (*She coughs*) Whoo, pardon me! Hairball! (*She coughs again, and as she does so, she disappears*)

DOLORES: (*Disembodied voice*) See you in the morning, Kiddo! Bright and early . . . At the studio!

Sam rolls her eyes, and stops to look in the mirror. She places her hands on her hips and mimics Dolores.

SAM: . . . 'This *much* Jazz Diva into *that much* Juvenile Delinquent, nyah nyah nyah!' (*She shudders at the memory of being possessed by Dolores*) Yuk!

She crosses to the radio and turns it on.

DJ: . . . And moving all the way up to the number one slot, in its first week in the chart, is the latest biggie from the Buggy. That man Bug Daddy B has done it again. You wanted it, so here it is: 'Suburban Ghetto Smackdown Jam', from the man himself.

The track begins to play.

SAM: Oh no you don't!

She quickly switches the radio off. The door knocks again.

SAM: Come in.

PAUL: (*Entering*) Sam, when you do the laundry, could you wash my new shirt?

He holds up shirt, to reveal it covered in lollipops.

Perhaps we should explain, not by way of excusing ourselves, but to put what you have just read in context, *Stage Fright* was our first collective foray into sitcom writing, after years of writing plays, TV comedy material and sketch shows, and books both solo and with other partners. The first thing you may have noticed, if you have been studying other sitcom scripts, is the length. Although we all tend to think of and refer to sitcoms as 'half hours', they are considerably shorter than that. Watching an episode of *Friends* from the first series on video the other day, it was noted that it actually ran at 21 minutes from opening to end credits, excluding commercial break. A BBC script generally runs at 28 minutes, whereas an ITV or Channel 4 script runs for 24 minutes. As we mentioned in the first chapter, when writing for children's series, you have to keep the scenes short and snappy. In this first draft, as much because we were working through the story as because we were unfamiliar with the form, the scenes tend to be relatively long. When working on subsequent series for children, not to mention subsequent drafts of *Stage Fright* (as you will see in a moment) it became second nature to write shorter scenes than we would for 'adult' series.

Another aspect of writing for the different broadcasters is the fact that when writing for the ITV companies, you have to tailor your script to accommodate a 'cliffhanger' ending to take you into the commercial break. The idea of this, of course, is to keep the viewer hooked and less willing to turn over to the snooker highlights or that documentary about the Hungarian basket weavers' convention. This does mean, however, that when writing your script, you do effectively have to build to two climaxes in your story, and with four minutes less time to do it in than on the BBC.

Let's show you a later draft of the same episode of *Stage Fright*, and compare the two.

Stage Fright Episode 6

Please Don't Talk About Me When I'm Gone

By John Byrne & Marcus Powell

Scene One: 'SWITCHED-ON TV'.
Jamie the presenter of 'SWITCHED-ON TV', a cable TV 'youth' programme is winding up another show. Behind him, the credits to a cartoon are rolling.

JAMIE:　　　Wicked! There'll be more cartoon craziness from 'The Disco Witch' and 'Pop-Cat' on 'Switched-On TV' next week.

(He indicates two giant witch and cat figures behind him)

JAMIE: *(cont)* And live on the show, the Megapop-alicious Bug Daddy B. We're gonna leave you with his latest vid, so 'til next time, I'm Jamie, and I'm outta here, but you stay – 'Switched On!'

The screen dissolves into a music video: Bug Daddy B is dressed in Gangsta rapper outfit i.e., long white coat, suit and hat to match, dark glasses and a gold-topped cane, flanked by half-a-dozen female dancers.

BUG DADDY B: *(rapping)* I jumped upon the bus and tried to pay half fare,

but the conductor grabbed me by my under-wear.

I said: 'D'You know who I am? My name is Bug Daddy B.'

He said: 'Wow, I've just been playing your new CD.'

So he let me go, apologised for the fuss.

I gave him my autograph – Guess what?

He gave me the bus!

A 1940s swing band style sample and scat vocal chorus cuts in, and we see the silhouette of a woman singing at a microphone.

Scene Two: STAGE SCHOOL CANTEEN.
Sam, Jools and Fitz in the Stacey Parrish Academy canteen watching Jamie's show . . . until Patience switches it off.

PATIENCE: Do you mind? I'm *trying* to talk to my beauty therapist *(into mobile)* Laurent?

JOOLS: Hey! We were watching that video! It's the lick – Bug Daddy B!

SAM: Leave it, Jools. We don't want to keep Patience's beauty therapist on hold. Plasterers charge a lot per hour.

PATIENCE: Ha Ha! Well, they certainly earn more than shabby junk shop owners like your dad. I'm surprised you're wasting your school fees watching TV.

Sam gets up to thump her, but Jools manages to step in.

JOOLS: Actually, Patience, this is research.

Patience gives a 'What are you babbling on about?' look. Fitz, meanwhile, is ever anxious for her attention.

FITZ: 'Switched-On TV'! We're all working behind the scenes next week. Our work experience placement, remember . . . ?

PATIENCE: BEHIND the scenes? We'll see. (*Finally gets through on her mobile*) Laurent? Book me in for all day Saturday. (*To Sam and Jools*) I'm a front of camera girl.

She swans out.

SAM: (*calling after her*) Yeah – but only if we were working on *Animal Hospital*!!

Scene Three: SAM'S BEDROOM. EVENING
Typical teenager's bedroom – clothes everywhere. Sam's sorting through her drawer. She takes a blouse and 'models' it for the cat sitting on her bed.

SAM: Here Tibby: Does this say 'rising young media executive'? (*Pause*) Yes, I think so too. No good for 'Switched-on TV' then. Wonder what I've got in my wardrobe that says 'trendy dogsbody'?

As she shuts her drawer, she hears Dolores' voice inside.

DOLORES: Hold on a minute there, Missy.

SAM: Dolores?

DOLORES: No, this is the voice of your underwear. Of course it's me.

She floats out of the drawer before stretching to full size. She is dressed in a red sparkling evening gown. She is wearing dark glasses, has a lei around her neck, and a suitcase with the initials C.N.C.S. stuck on the side.

SAM:	Where have you been? I haven't seen you all week.
DOLORES:	On vacation. At the Cloud Nine Celestial Spa. Shakespeare was there.
SAM:	You met William Shakespeare?
DOLORES:	Oh yeh! Nice guy. Sure talks funny, but he plays a mean game of Scrabble. And I also learnt this groovy new trick from Harry Houdini, the magician . . .

Just then they're interrupted by a knock on the door.

SAM:	Come in.

It's Paul, with shirts and clothes in hand.

DOLORES:	Well heeellllloooo, 'High, Wide and Handsome'.
PAUL:	Hi Sam. Ready to knock 'em dead tomorrow?
SAM:	Dad, I told you, I'm not on screen, I'm just working at the studio.

Dolores registers surprise.

PAUL:	Well, who have they got on the show this week, then?
SAM:	Would you believe Bug Daddy B? Jools is over the moon.
PAUL:	Bug Daddy? Hey! I like him. (*He performs an embarrassing version of Bug Daddy B's lyrics*)

'I jumped upon the bus.

I tried to do my rap,

but I fell into an old lady's lap . . . '

SAM:	(*to herself*) Oh my God!
PAUL:	' . . . She hit me on the head

With a bip and a bop,

So I hip hopped off at the next bus stop.'

SAM:	That's . . . er . . . cool, Dad.

DOLORES: I don't know what that was . . . But he sure looked good doing it!

Dolores leaps into the body of the cat sitting on the bed. The 'cat' then leaps into the arms of Paul, and begins purring. From Sam's point of view we see Dolores in Paul's arms, smiling contentedly.

PAUL: I don't know what's got into this cat of yours lately. (*He places the cat gently on the bed*). Okay, you're on laundry, I'm doing dinner . . .

Paul exits. Dolores leaps out of the cat's body and appears next to Sam. The cat lets out a strangulated 'Meeeoooowww!' shakes its head, and runs out. Sam stares at Dolores, stunned.

DOLORES: Classy, huh? That's the trick Houdini showed me!

SAM: But how did you . . . ?

Dolores leaps into Sam and poses in front of the mirror.

SAM: (*with Dolores' voice*) Never mind me – how can YOU wear these clothes?

Dolores leaps back out of Sam's body.

SAM: Yuk! Don't EVER do that again!

She starts to sort out Paul's shirts. As Dolores is talking, Sam finds a letter in his shirt pocket and begins reading.

DOLORES: It was no picnic for me either, Lamb Chop. Squeezing *this much* Jazz Diva into *that much* Juvenile Delinquent isn't my idea of a swingin' time. (*She notices Sam's change of mood*) What's up?

SAM: It's from Dad's bank. If his takings don't improve this summer they're going to close him down.

DOLORES: I'm sorry kid. Hey, cheer up – things will improve. Trust me, I can feel it in my ectoplasm. So, what time do we hit the TV studio?

SAM: What do you mean 'we'? Over my dead body!

DOLORES: I think you mean *my* dead body – and don't worry kid – it's gonna be floating right along with you, so don't touch that dial!

Well, as you will probably have noticed, the first thing we addressed was the length of the scenes, not to mention the dialogue contained within them. In the first draft we included a female presenter in the opening scene, who by the time of the later draft, had completely disappeared. This was as much to do with financial considerations as narrative ones – less actors, less wages – but, again, these are all things that have to be considered from draft to draft. A script that contains six central characters and five locations, may end up with three central characters and four locations by the final draft, with one of your characters changing from teenage boy to 30-something female, and one of your locations suddenly becoming an off-licence instead of a library.

The first and second scenes were condensed, resulting in a shortened version of the rap. Scene Two in the later version is radically different from the first draft, with the inclusion of Sam's nemesis Patience, (she does appear in the original draft script, but not until a later scene) and the exclusion of Stacey Parrish the school Principal. The running visual gag of the boy getting constantly covered in food has been dropped, not to mention Fitz's appearance in the Pop-Cat costume. In terms of the dialogue, most of the lines from the first version were cut, and those that remain tend to be considerably shortened (if you find yourself working with a producer or script editor who likes to be 'hands-on', you may also find that some of your dialogue gets rewritten completely). In this script some changes were made at the 'request' of the producer, others were our own decision, some we agreed with, some we didn't, but this is all a part of the collaborative process, the way the business works.

Still want to write sitcoms for a living . . . ? If your answer to this is 'yes', then good for you, because despite all these hurdles (and if you think we've been exaggerating about some of the hoops you will potentially be put through – we're not!) the rewards can be tremendous – fame and fortune if you are one of the very lucky ones – but we were thinking more specifically of the reward you get from knowing that you have finally, truly finished writing your script . . . until the next time!

7. Selling your sitcom

As every experienced comedy writer knows, you can have written the greatest sitcom in the world and it won't do you any good if you can't bring it to everyone else's attention. If you've been busy working through the other chapters of this book, you may not have written quite the best script in the world – but you should certainly have a fairly decent one, and at last it's time to share it with a wider world. Or more to the point, with the movers and shakers in the broadcast industry who can bridge that gap between you and the wider world (and hopefully pay you well for the privilege).

So if you've got a fresh copy of your script off the printer, and your courage in both hands let's . . . well, actually let's not leap into the selling process immediately until we've discussed a few important points about the salesperson: you.

Bypass the writing section in any bookshop and browse further into the (usually much larger) section on sales and marketing techniques. Just as comedy writers have different styles, your approach to selling is a matter of personal taste too. If you're part of a comedy writing team, one of you may be better at this area than the other . . . but it's still a good idea for both of you to put your heads together to come up with creative (but professional) ways of selling your work. Later in this chapter we'll say a word or two about agents and 'contacts' but the bottom line is that YOU are the only one who really believes strongly enough in your ability to sell it to the rest of the world.

Of course it's also true that there will be quite a few other writers out there who believe in themselves just as strongly and are vying for the very same slots. That's why playing to our strengths and knowing our weaknesses is just as important when we're marketing a script as when we're writing it.

116

Strengths and weaknesses can often be closely related. For some of us it's the thought of seeing our work up there on the screen, and the fame and fortune that will (hopefully) follow that motivates us to get our work out there in the first place. As long as we are prepared to actually put some work in, a strong clear vision of the end result can be a really powerful driver to get that script written and out there in double quick time. But if speed and focus is your strength, just be sure you give your script an extra 'once over' before you send it off. In our eagerness to share our masterpiece with its audience, it's not unknown for the occasional plot hiccup or spelling error to creep in, and the first requirement of effective marketing is that you've got to have top quality product to market.

Then there's the other kind of writer – the one who actually enjoys the writing process. Quality sitcoms come from working on jokes and situations over and over again until every line is a gem – trouble is, for them sometimes perfection is never quite perfect enough. If that sounds like you, bear in mind that sometimes scripts and ideas we hold back from pushing out into the world 'until they are ready' never make it to 'ready' at all . . . and sitcoms which aren't half as good get commissioned because the writers had the courage to actually send them out there.

Which begs the question of where 'out there' is. The good news is that if you've been doing your homework as a writer throughout this book, you've also done quite a lot of your homework as a marketeer.

At the beginning of the book we encouraged you to research as many top quality sitcoms as possible, initially with a view to working on the quality of your script content – but we hope, particularly with contemporary sitcoms, that you were also paying attention to the names of producers, directors and production companies that feature in the end credits of these shows. What channels did you watch or listen to these sitcoms on? Were there particular timeslots the shows were aired in? Who are the commissioning editors for comedy for those channels (and is the sitcom commissioner different from the comedy editor?) Who are the current hot sitcom stars? Or are there supporting actors in existing sitcoms who look like they are making a big enough impression to spin off into their own shows?

All of these people are your potential leads and gatekeepers to target with your sitcom script and proposal. As we've already noted, you'll be able to find many of the names by keeping a close eye on the credits at the end of the shows themselves. Other names you'll become familiar with by reading the broadcast trade press, the media pages of the national papers and, if all else fails, by phoning the duty offices of the TV and radio stations and asking. We've put a comprehensive list of resources at the end of the book but any list you yourself build is bound to be more effective as it will reflect your own preferences and the style of comedy that most appeals to you. As with selling any other commodity, one of the best ways of knowing what your sitcom audience likes is to be part of that audience yourself.

Be particularly alert for changes of TV executives (the new person in the job may well be looking for new show ideas to establish their name), for TV production companies joining the hallowed ranks of 'preferred providers' for the big channels, and for major bankable stars who quit popular programmes for new horizons and may be looking for a new vehicle. Your sitcom may be just what the doctor ordered – not to mention the ex-police, detective or veterinary drama star.

Contacts and agents

One of the reasons we often hear sitcom writers give for lack of success is 'not having the right contacts'. There's a strong belief that TV is a closed shop, run by university graduates, a London clique or refugees from the 1980s alternative comedy circuit who only ever give jobs out to their mates. It's certainly undeniable that if you could just pick up the phone and call the right people things might move a lot quicker, and given that the world of media is becoming more and more celebrity and gossip orientated, we might even reluctantly concede that for a comic actor or actress, becoming a regular on the nightclub circuit and providing exciting pics for the paparazzi may be a more direct route to primetime TV success than a whole programme of RADA courses. However, writers, even the more successful ones, tend to be slightly less photogenic creatures than the starlets, so ultimately the building blocks of success are still well-crafted words on the page, rather then the well-crafted works of the plastic surgeon. It's just getting your pages in front of the right people that's the challenge.

As for the 'London Clique' charge – well, it's certainly true that it's easier to break into the media if you live and work in the media capital, but the recent success of comedy shows like *The Grimleys* and *Phoenix Nights* show that a strong local flavour (as long as it's accompanied by an equally strong script) can break through cultural and geographic barriers. The modern classic *Father Ted*, which on the one hand seemed quintessentially Irish, not to mention Catholic, in flavour, sold very successfully worldwide and obviously struck a chord with audiences everywhere from China to Iceland.

Even if you don't sell your sitcom the first time – and instant success comes to very few serious writers, if your work is good enough somebody will take notice, even if it's only to send you a note saying 'not this time, but keep trying'. If your name keeps turning up in people's inboxes and mail trays (always accompanied by work worth looking at, of course) it will start to become familiar. Make it your business to reply courteously and keep in contact with anyone who takes the time to respond to your work: slowly but surely you're building your own list of contacts.

Speaking of contacts brings us to the subject of agents and it's certainly an attractive idea for most writers to have someone else take on the hard slog of selling their work, especially someone who already has lots of contacts in the industry. Unfortunately the only reason an agent is likely to take on your work is if they feel they can make money out of it, so like it or not you still have a selling job to do.

Bear in mind also that the top agents already have the top writers on their books – and are likely to work harder for existing clients and the larger cheques they bring in than beginning writers who being untried, will earn less initially. Having said that, a smart agent will be on the lookout for a writer, writing team or sitcom which has the *potential* to become the next big thing. So your approach to an agent needs to be just as polished as the package you would send to a top TV or radio company.

Now let's look at what you need to have in that package:

1. Your series proposal

If you are pitching a brand new sitcom, you will need to set out in an exciting, attention-grabbing way, the basic premise of your sitcom, the characters and most of all, what is unique and attractive about it from the audience's point of view. You can write this proposal either before or after you have actually written a script, and different writers will recommend one or the other method. Some writers insist on developing the script first – after all, an idea can change a lot from its original concept while being executed. Others like to write the proposal first as a vision statement to help crystalise the show idea in their minds and give a finished product to work towards. If you are writing in advance it can be useful to fantasize that the show already exists and that you are writing a review of it for a paper or magazine. It's surprising how much you will 'know' about your show even before you write it . . . it's also surprising how many unforseen plotholes come up when you're trying to get it all down in this way. The example below is a proposal for *Power Games* a teenage sitcom about two children whose mum suddenly becomes a high ranking minister. Note that the initial concept is explained in the first few lines and then expanded later. Just like TV viewers you have to catch the potential producer's attention before they have a chance to switch off.

Do some role play and put yourself in the producer's mind – what would you like to know about a show if a beginning writer is asking you to invest in it? In the *Power Games* proposal there's a location list to show that even though it's set in high places, it won't be too difficult to shoot, as well as a snatch of an opening rap to fill in the back story each week, *Fresh Prince* style.

2. The script?

That question mark is there for a reason – it's debatable whether you should send a script with the original proposal. On the one hand the people you are approaching are busy so they may be much more likely to take time to read a one or two page pitch than wade through a full script. If they then want to see a script, you can at least send it in the confidence that it's going to someone who is actually interested in reading it. On the other hand, if a strong idea is also accompanied by a good script, it certainly encourages the producer that the project is worth taking to the next stage.

There is certainly no question that regardless of whether you send it with the initial package, you should have the script either written or at least mapped out in your head so you can turn it around pretty quickly. After all, the logical next step for a producer who likes your proposal is to ask to see a script and it hardly creates a good impression if they then have to wait a month for you to write it . . . or if you dash something off which doesn't do justice to the original idea.

3. Storylines
The proposal is interesting. The script is well written. By now the producer will have two ideas in their head. One will be 'This idea looks like it's worth investing in.' Number two will be 'What's likely to go wrong if I invest in this idea?' Depending on how high up the producer is in the company, thought number two can sometimes be a lot stronger than thought number one!

One of the principal fears about beginning or untried writers is that while they can do one good script as a fluke, the idea or their ability to work with it won't be sustainable. Providing at least six well thought out storylines, preferably showing the versatility of the premise and characters is a good way of addressing this fear.

4. The letter
This comes last in the list, but it's actually the most important part of the package because it's what the reader will see first. It should be short and businesslike, telling the producer what your idea is, why you think it will appeal to viewers and a little bit about who you are. If you haven't any previous sitcom credits but you have had success in other areas of writing, by all means put that in briefly. Equally, if you are a complete beginner simply state that you have an idea they may be interested in commissioning and let your product speak for itself. Avoid sounding either arrogant or desperate and *under no circumstances try to sound funny.* You are ultimately asking

someone to invest a substantial sum of money in your work – you need to show them you take it as seriously as they do.

Which brings us to a further point about your package: you can find all kinds of humour in sitcoms, ranging from highly sophisticated and adult to utterly childish. Sometimes you can find both kinds in the same show. The next few paragraphs may seem to come from the childish end of the spectrum, not to say downright patronising. Nevertheless, we have seen enough promising projects scuppered by forgetting this basic rule to convince us that it's well worth emphasising, and even over-emphasising: NOBODY IS GOING TO RESPECT YOUR WORK IF YOU DON'T SHOW YOU RESPECT IT IN THE FIRST PLACE. What do we mean by this? Surely it's obvious that you have respect for your own work – after all, you and/or your writing partner will have spent long hours getting it to the stage when it's worth sending off. Sadly, it may be precisely because the average writer spends long hours cooped up by themselves, that basic presentation rules get left by the wayside.

For instance, we still occasionally see scripts which are handwritten. In this day and age there's just no way such a submission is going to be taken seriously. You might be Neil Simon, Richard Curtis and Galton and Simpson all rolled into one, but the people you are pitching your scripts to are too busy to battle with your handwriting to find that out – and no, it doesn't matter how neat your handwriting is.

If you can't or won't type yourself, hire someone else to do it for you.

(At the other end of the spectrum, the rule about people being too busy to fight their way past messy or unclear submissions also applies – you may have the most sophisticated state-of-the-art computer money can buy . . . but if your printer ink starts to run out halfway through turning out your script, any good impression will immediately be thrown away. Even more common is the submission sent in on computer disk or via e-mail . . . only the writer hasn't bothered to check whether they are using a system that is compatable with the one the person they are submitting to uses. Most major companies discourage unsolicited submissions via e-mail anyhow. Besides the fact that there are confidentiality and copyright issues, an unsolicited script could very easily contain a computer virus and is highly likely to be deleted without ever being opened.)

Assuming your script is legible, another major flaw of first-time submissions is bad spelling and worse grammar. The fact that it's a comedy script is no excuse – you are aiming to present yourself as a professional so if these areas aren't your strong points, get someone who *is* strong on these areas to give your package the once over before you close the envelope.

Oh yes, the envelope . . . please, please, please use a decent-sized one which can hold your script and accompanying material comfortably and is reasonably resilient. Everyone likes to think they are being offered a script which is exclusive and hot off the presses . . . if your script arrives crumpled and be-draggled having suffered the worst the postal journey has to offer, it doesn't really help the impression. Should you include a stamped addressed return envelope? We know some writers who don't do so on the grounds that it's inviting rejection . . . we prefer to believe it shows that you respect and care about your work and that if this particular person doesn't want to commission it you are confident someone else will.

Certainly we have seen all the above errors of presentation made often enough to suggest that your chances of standing out from the crowd are immediately increased simply by taking a bit of time to get the physical presentation of your work right.

And once you have checked off all these pointers and put the script in the post what happens next?

Well, a number of things may happen. The most likely of which is NOTHING for a long time. Now we know just how frustrating that can be – after all part of the excitement of writing a sitcom script is thinking ahead to the giggles and guffaws and general hilarity that is going to ensue once you share your witty words with the world at large. So it can be a real let down if you don't get a call back in a day or so to say the TV company or production outfit has stopped everything once they saw your masterpiece and wants to offer you an immediate commission. In all honesty it's unlikely they'll even have read your script in such a short time. Most TV executives and producers already have shows ongoing and that's where they'll be directing most of their attention even if they've already asked to see your show. If the submission is unsolicited you can expect an even longer wait – some major comedy production companies report that they receive at least two or three unsolicited scripts every week, which go into a growing slush pile until someone has time to go through them.

What you should get after a couple of weeks though, is some acknowledgement that your script has been received. It will usually be accompanied by a release form which the company will insist you sign before they will even look at your material. The release form absolves the company of any liability if they or someone associated with them should produce a show later on which you might be able to claim was ripped off from your idea.

Name any big hit show, book, film or song of the past decade and the chances are someone somewhere has filed a lawsuit claiming they were the ones who thought of the idea, so you can't blame the companies for being a bit wary. Equally it's not unknown for the same idea to crop up over and over again and independently to different writers as we saw when we were brainstorming sitcom ideas at the beginning of the book. And no, we're not naive enough to believe that sitcom ideas don't get ripped off from beginning writers from time to time.

We know only one guaranteed iron clad way to make sure nobody steals your idea and that's never to send them anywhere (and we know some very promising writers who seem to have adopted that very technique, which is why you've never heard of them). For most of us, taking sensible copyright precautions such as mailing a copy of the script to ourselves and leaving it unopened is protection enough. And as we have noted, it's unlikely a company will agree to read your script without you first signing that release form. Some instructors even suggest that writers pre-empt the release form by typing up one of their own and including it with the original package . . . don't be surprised if you still get the company's official one back in the post though.

If you hear nothing from the people you've sent your show to after about a month, it can certainly be worth a phone call to check that the parcel actually arrived, but harassing the company (and especially the receptionist) for comments or feedback is likely to do far more harm then good. If they like your stuff someone will get back to you eventually.

What should you be doing in the meantime? Well, you might want to work on other sitcom ideas – after all, it's a career as a comedy writer rather then one quick hit that you're aiming to build (more about this in Chapter 8). Should you send your existing sitcom to a few more companies? Well, there are two perspectives on this one. Some writers and producers feel that TV is so cut-throat that every company likes to feel they have the 'exclusive' on a new project even if they choose to reject it later. So knowing that other companies are looking at the same project may put them off. Other writers and agents feel that if the sitcom is any good, knowing other companies might grab it first will encourage producers to move quickly. It's certainly true that bidding wars stoked by astute agents have become a common phenomenon of the book trade recently, even over new writers.

One good reason for having multiple submissions, whether of the same or different sitcoms, out in the market at the same time is that if one proposal does get rejected, there are other possibilities out there to keep your spirits up.

Make no mistake – getting rejected is never fun no matter how long you have been working in the writing business. Especially if you've spent long hours turning out a 30-minute script and all you get back in the post is a brief pre-printed note telling you your hard work is 'not what we require at this time'. By all means feel the pain but don't take it out on your family (and especially not on your writing partner), and whatever you do, don't necessarily conclude that you're not cut out for the writing business. Most successful writers have experienced rejection, often multiple rejections, in the early part of their careers. Many of us still have the odd project knocked back, and believe us, it doesn't feel any nicer no matter how many successes we have under our belt.

But there are many reasons why a script may be rejected which are entirely independent of its quality. The company may have something very similar in production or under offer already (like we said, ideas are more common than we like to think); even more likely, the company may be aware that someone else in the industry has something similar in production. Humour is a very subjective thing, so the particular style of humour in your sitcom may not appeal to the person you're pitching to. John recently had a humorous cookery show turned down by a producer who thought it was a perfectly viable idea, but just personally didn't like cookery (any offers from producers who DO like cookery, care of the publisher please!)

Commissioning editors often have shopping lists of programmes they would like and programmes they specifically don't want, which are shared with the production companies but not the general public – if your programme idea happens to fall into the wrong list, the production company won't want to invest in it no matter what the quality of the idea. (Of course commissioning editors can suddenly change their minds, or be changed themselves if they have too many dud commissions, so don't be at all surprised if a programme idea of yours which gets rejected one year looks a lot like something else which gets commissioned a few years later. Unless you pitched it to the same production company of course. If you've already signed the release form though you'll have to chalk it up to experience.)

So what happens if you are one of the lucky few who get a positive response to your submission? Congratulations . . . but you're not out of the woods yet.

It's very unlikely that the production company will want to commission your script exactly as it is, no matter how much they like it, and especially if you are a new writer.

What will normally happen is that you will be invited in for a meeting to discuss your idea. This is a very exciting prospect for any new writer. Besides the fact that visions of huge sums of money may fill your head (visions which you can quickly forget if it's a radio sitcom or a pilot that's on offer!), getting a meeting is an indication that you may be getting somewhere and the long hours of slogging away at the computer screen may actually have been worth it.

Remember though that this meeting is just that – a meeting. The company may be interested in your sitcom but need you to really sell them on why they should invest in developing it further. It may be that they want to see how professional a writer you are in general – obviously there's no point in them commissioning something that doesn't have series potential and getting tied up with a new writer who isn't capable of developing the show past one episode. It may also be that they are not so much interested in the particular idea you sent but have some other project they want you to work on.

By all means, therefore, know your sitcom inside out and be fully conversant with all the reasons why it would be sustainable as a hit series and why you are just the writer to write it, but at the same time remember the old adage that we have twice as many ears as we have mouths. If you are part of a comedy partnership or team be particularly careful about how you come across in the meeting. Talking over one another is very unlikely to help your professional image.

It's best to work out in advance who is strongest on which area of the script and will therefore answer questions on that aspect. If one member of the team is better at talking than others, that's fine too – as long as there are no big rows about who said what or who should have said what after the meeting.

Assuming the producer is interested in taking the series idea further, the issues at the forefront of his or her mind are likely to be very practical ones – can you work professionally and meet deadlines, have you got enough ideas to sustain a series or even a couple of series if the show is successful? But superceding all of these questions will be the question of how easy you are to work with. It's stressful enough working with established writers without bringing in a new one to add to the stress.

Your professional image can be enhanced by knowing your sitcom inside out – not just the scripts you have written already or the plotlines you have included with your proposal – but being able to talk about your characters in detail and suggest how they could grow and develop and perform in scenarios that the producer may suggest. They may also have suggestions on changes to your original idea and this is where the 'being easy to work with' element comes in.

You've worked hard on your series idea and your script and it is perfectly natural and admirable to view it as 'your baby'. The nature of bringing it to a production company though, means that it is no longer going to be exclusively your baby, and most producers will want to make sure the show suits their requirements and the requirements of the networks they are planning to sell it on to. If the company is a credible one, and particularly if it has a track record in comedy (you should have researched the company before making the submission, of course), there is a chance they may have an inside track on some of the latest requirements on those commissioning 'shopping lists' and tweaking your sitcom outline a little may make it even more attractive then before.

Your strategy in the discussion should be to keep your ears and your mind open, listening to any suggestions. Ultimately it's up to you to decide whether you take them or not, but don't be so busy defending your work that you miss hearing them altogether.

You may or may not get a decision on whether the producer wants to go ahead straight after the meeting. In some cases the producer may want to consider the idea further before making an offer – you may even be asked to redo the proposal based on things that have come up in the meeting. It's also possible that the person you are meeting may not have the ultimate decision. Don't pester is the golden rule – but don't put your life on hold either. If they are interested you'll hear back sooner rather then later – or they will contact you to explain why there's a delay.

One caution: the meeting could go extremely well, the producer obviously loves your show and laughs at all your jokes, in fact the two of you brainstorm lots more ideas for plotlines and discuss the big stars who will definitely be approached to play the lead roles . . . and then you never hear from the company again.

That, as they say, is showbiz. It may be that you've just met one of the 'big talkers/no actioners' who are common in the industry, but it may also be that the interest was very genuine. Unfortunately, if a week is a long time in politics, a day can be a lifetime in the entertainment media. A similar show could have been pronounced a flop, the commissioning editor for comedy at one of the networks may have changed and be looking for a whole new kind of project. The producer could have been sacked or moved on – there are a whole range of situations which can arise to scupper your sitcom commission at the last minute.

Such disappointments can be hard to deal with, but they go with the territory. The only way to deal with them is to keep writing and know that you will laugh about it someday. Or in our case write about it in your book.

Pick yourself up, dust yourself off and start writing and pitching all over again – and sooner or later you WILL get the magical offer letter through the post.

Consider the offer carefully (and take a look at our advice in the last chapter about contracts) and then allow yourself a small celebration of getting this near to your goal. And in the next chapter we'll take the rest of the journey as we look at the progress of you and your sitcom from script to studio floor to screen and beyond.

Sample proposal:

Power Games

The teen sitcom that rocks and rules by John Byrne

Single mum **Marcia Power** has just been made Minister of Education after a barn-storming campaign helped deliver a landslide victory in the General Election. Her kids, **Kelli** and **Carl,** who must have knocked on every door in Handsworth to make it happen, suddenly find themselves whisked off to London.

Kelli's got her mum's gift for straight talking and Carl reckons his MC-ing skills really swung it with the hipper voters. But while a posh new flat and hobnobbing with the stars may be the perks of this new life, being 'role models for the Nation's Yout' is kind of strange for two kids who've made a life out of keeping things real. Kelli and Carl are well used to coping with the inner city, but the inner circle of the wealthy and powerful is a whole new ball game.

Or as Carl tells it in the opening titles (cut to spoof news footage and press cuttings):

My Mum was a teacher in a really tough school

But she sorted it out and made everything cool,

Then our whole lives moved in a different direction

'Cos Mum decided to stand for election.

She really kicked butt, won the seat and then

My Mama got a call from Big Daddy PM

Who said 'Yo! you gotta come and Save the Nation'

Now my Mama's in charge of education.

And we livin' it large cause that's part of the deal,

Tho' me and my sis are tryin' to keep things real.

Got a new posh posse, kids of big shot peeps –

Yo, they're just like us when you look beneath –

But it's hard in the hood to keep your cred in the frame

When you're trapped at the top playing POWER GAMES!

Marcia gets embroiled in some really sticky political situations, and Kelli and Carl are torn between sticking by her, sticking with their new friends and sticking to their own opinions.

Power Games is a show that will satirise politics from kids' perspective. It'll be sharp, telling, funny and intriguing – and sometimes will show that running the country is a cinch compared to running teenage life according to plan.

Regular locations and characters:
The Powers' new flat is at the top of a Government building in Whitehall which also houses:

- a gym and fitness club for ministers and civil servants over the rank of Sub-assistant Under Secretary;

- a drivers' and bodyguards' staffroom;

- an underground tunnel to Number Ten, where **Andy Cameron**, 'the People's PM' lives with his family;

- and the extensive offices of 'Communications HQ', presided over by oily spin doctor, **Robert Thorpe**, a man who sees Marcia's sudden rise as a threat to his close relationship with the PM and **Nadia Hussain**, his stylish, ambitious (but scrupulous) Number Two.

Exploring their new world, Kelli and Carl soon come into contact with:

- **Hugh**, the PM's angst-ridden son who desperately wants a normal teenage life ('How can I organise an underground garage party when our garage is full of Special Branch?');

- **Melody Flute**, Hugh's ditsy American megastar girlfriend, who keeps in touch by e-mail and videolink when she's not in town;

- **Shirin Hussain,** Nadia's niece who's definitely junior spin doctor material, and determined to run rings round her family;

- and SAS-trained hunk **Carlton Robinson,** Marcia's newly-assigned driver who's very put out by the family's enthusiasm for London Transport, and has uncharacteristically tender feelings for his new boss.

Story ideas:

Through Carl and Kelli, this new 'posh posse' is about to learn some tricks from the mean streets, while our reluctant heroes learn that politics isn't just all talk – in fact, they're usually right in the thick of the action!

Like when . . .

- A teacher's strike over discipline threatens and Marcia steps in to help resolve it. Her position isn't helped very much when Kelli's sharp tongue gets her kicked out of school!

- Robert Thorpe is being wined and dined by a multi-national company that's cutting down whole swathes of the West African rainforest. Enter Marcia's 'Aunt Funke' on a holiday from Nigeria . . .

- The Cabinet is deeply divided on the Defence Budget when the kids discover a secret bunker deep in the bowels of Whitehall designed for use in time of National Crisis. National Crisis promptly ensues when Carl and Hugh set up their own pirate radio station down there, featuring MC Peace.

- When a young prince's behaviour starts giving cause for concern, who better to mentor him than the kids of the Education Minister, the Prime Minister and the niece of a top spin doctor? Almost anybody it seems, when our heroes manage to cram a whole 'annus horribilus' into one outdoor weekend.

- Marcia is making a brave stand against the PM's pet scheme to introduce ID cards for teenagers. Then she discovers Carl and Kelli have blagged their way into an over-18s music venue. She starts to waver on the issue, until Kelli suggests they take Hugh along next time.

8. From Script to Screen

So you have a commission! Congratulations (in advance, if you're reading ahead in the book and haven't actually finished your sample sitcom script yet!)

In this chapter we're going to take you on a journey through the various things that happen up to and during filming from a writer's point of view. Naturally every project and production company is different, so everything may not always happen as we've laid it out here and even if it does, it may not necessarily happen in this order.

However, the nature of sitcoms, and especially series production, means that certain systems have developed which most production companies tend to adhere to. If you know what to expect, even as a beginning writer it shouldn't be too difficult to come across as being a little more professional than you actually feel. More to the point, your ultimate goal should be to establish a good reputation in the business so that you get to work on more sitcom projects and also establish more creative control over the ones you do work on.

When you, the producer and the script editor (not to mention their wives/husbands, families and anyone else they choose to consult) are finally happy with the script, the production moves on to the next stage – a script reading with the actors, and the director too. For most writers this is an exciting stage of the process, as it's the first chance to see the words you've written brought to life by professionals. Even if you've done the test readings we suggested in the chapters on the writing process, some of the words may come to life in a very different way than you expected when you wrote them.

If you're a comedy fan (and even if you weren't before you started this book we hope you are by now), you'll be particularly thrilled to see your work performed by seasoned comedy actors you'll recognise from other shows. Or at least you will if the producer is in the mood to play safe.

The general direction of TV (and increasingly radio) today is that the 'stars' tend to be the younger more photogenic players, and whether or not you wrote your sitcom with particular stars in mind, considering whether there's a place in your show for one of these 'hot properties' will certainly have been a factor in the producer's mind before deciding to invest in it.

However, in addition to the 'celebs', there are also some very experienced comedy and character actors available and hopefully a few of them will have been cast in your show. You may find you don't know the names unless you're a real dyed-in-the-wool comedy buff, but you will certainly know their faces from supporting roles in TV shows, films and adverts.

There have been many attempts to build sitcoms around successful stand-up comedians and latterly around popular TV presenters, but with a few exceptions these types of project don't usually work. For one thing, stand-ups and presenters usually excel at being themselves (albeit exaggerated versions of themselves) in front of live audiences. Working to a script and interacting with other performers can be a very different experience for them. Stand-ups who are successful in both mediums tend to be the ones who have some sort of drama background, while many of the supporting actors we associate with comedy on TV often have long careers in dramatic theatre when they are off camera. A good example was the late Sir Nigel Hawthorne who became famous as the Machiavellian civil servant Sir Humphry in *Yes, Minister* after spending as he put it 'sixty years on stage becoming an overnight success'.

Good actors won't just read through your script, they will add something to it. In some cases this will happen as soon as they pick up the script and get into character. Of course if they are seeing the script for the first time, they'll also hopefully laugh at the jokes which is always encouraging. (Don't be thrown however by some old pros who turn up at rehearsals looking disinterested and sometimes even comatose . . . we've seen some of these people pull amazing performances out of the bag when the lights go up and it's showtime for real.)

As the cast reads through the script, you, the script editor and the producer will be making notes. In some cases, it will be to note lines or scenes which don't work when read aloud and need to be changed. In other cases, hearing the characters speak may well give you ideas for new lines or gags which you'll be itching to add to your existing script. Remember though that professional actors by their nature like to have scripts learned well in advance – too many changes at the last minute won't go down very well no matter how funny the punchlines are. The opposite is also the case of course – every actor likes to have the funny lines in the show and you may be approached after the read by actors with suggestions for new lines to give their characters.

Some more forward performers will actually change your lines right in front of you. Control your desire to strangle them and remember the etiquette of TV production – if you have any comments for good or ill about particular performances, have a quiet word with the producer or director and get them to pass it on. If they respect your script enough to commission it in the first place, they should respect your opinions and take them seriously too. Of course, if you've balanced the script properly in the first place, the main protagonist may have the bulk of the gags, but there should be some laugh lines for the other actors too.

It's certainly true – and every actor's dream – that writers and producers have built up a small part in future episodes of a show because they like an actor's performance in the role. (On the other hand, for writers unused to the glamour of showbiz, perhaps we should caution you not to start giving a support character more and more lines because you've fallen madly in love with the actor or actress playing the part. Besides ruining your script, it will get you nowhere, since in terms of glamour, writers come somewhere in the pecking order below the studio cat.)

The art of comedy performing is timing and some comic actors are masters of the pause . . . sometimes so much so that you may even want to lose one of your existing lines to fit one in. You may also have to change lines and words around depending on the ways actors say them. Although you'll have written your script to fit an appropriate time slot, usually somewhere around the 30-minute mark, read throughs won't normally get done within the time. Don't worry too much if there's an overrun – unless the script is dramatically longer then necessary the director should be able to solve the problem with pacing or, if all else fails, in the final edit. Under-running is rarer, but more of a problem – if this happens you'll be asked to provide more material . . . but the read through itself should have given you ideas on what to expand.

Try to get an audio tape of the read through that you can refer to while rewriting (the producer will probably have arranged one anyway). If it's a radio sitcom, a tape is even more useful as you can listen to the words without being influenced by visuals which the eventual audience is never going to see.

After the read through, either immediately or when you have all had a chance to listen to the tape, you will sit down with the producer and script editor and compare notes on changes to the script. It would be nice to say that the next draft you write will be the final one, but there may well be several more rewrites to go before your script makes it to the studio floor (as mentioned in the previous chapter). And don't forget we're still talking about a pilot show here . . . imagine if you have been commissioned to write a whole series. And people wonder why the comedy industry is so keen on writers who work in pairs or on teams.

Depending on the time frame for recording the programme there may be a second read through with the new version of the script. This is the place where you may have to 'fight' politely for your work, as jokes which were funny when they were fresh start to lose their appeal when the cast have to read them over and over again. (This is not to suggest that every suggestion from an actor isn't useful. Some actors come up with great lines when improvising and if you watch reruns of classic shows like *Father Ted* or *Frasier*, you can often see that whereas in the first series, the actors were feeling their way into their characters, in the second or third series the writers are working to the strengths of the performers.)

So far we've been working on the assumption that the script you have been pitching and been commissioned to develop has been for a series of your own creation – still the norm in the British market. However, an increasing number of UK companies are trying to develop projects along the American model of hiring writers to work as part of a team on series they haven't necessarily created. If this opportunity arises for you (and it may well do off the back of an original series idea if it impresses the producers enough – good sitcom writers are rare enough that word spreads) the basic writing process will be the same but there are some significant differences and potential pitfalls you need to be aware of.

Unlike creating an idea for a series of your own, working as part of a script 'team' generally involves being brought in to script an idea from somebody else. This 'somebody else' may well not be a writer at all, but rather a researcher, producer, or even someone who works in the maintenance department. They do usually come from 'internal' sources, but it's not unheard of for a 'little old lady from Devon' to hit upon a good idea for a series and send it in. Broadcasters receive series ideas from all quarters but it generally falls to bona fide writers (You) to make those ideas work. Recently we had the experience of working on such a series.

Having been asked along to a meeting with the executive producer and the creator of the proposed series, we found ourselves presented with a proposal for a series which we, to be perfectly honest, didn't really like, and as such, had no problem in telling them that we didn't think it was particularly good. Of course, we had to temper this criticism with our own ideas on how to improve it. Our suggestions must have impressed them sufficiently, because a few days later, we were offered the job of writing the pilot, the creator having now effectively handed over the creative reins to us.

Fast forward four months, and the pilot script (eight rewrites later) is now completed. The pilot is given the go ahead to become a series of fifteen. However, any ideas of putting a down payment on a new car are swiftly scuppered when you realise that a whole team of other writers are now to be brought on board. To be fair, we knew this was going to be the case from the very beginning of the enterprise, but it does take some getting used to when you realise that 'your' script is now going to form the basis for a dozen other writers' work. Although, of course, all the writers worked on their individual episodes, there still had to be some uniformity to the scripts, which by now included several new characters created by us. However, don't think that your script is going to be taken as gospel, despite the fact that its commission is the reason for those other writers being there in the first place. Prepare to have everything you worked on, from character names, to plot choices – even your episode title, come under scrutiny. As it turned out, we went on to write another episode for the series, but had nothing whatsoever to do with the other writers' episodes, and as such, still have no idea what the series looked like as a whole. There were of course brainstorming sessions, where the new writers asked questions regarding character motivation etc, but ultimately, each writer's decision was their own (with a little help from the producer and script editor, of course). Incidentally, the creator never attended any of the meetings and we never saw them again.

On this kind of series, as opposed to a series you have created and worked on from scratch, you will find that things are taken out of your hands very quickly once you have completed your script. While writing, you may have certain ideas about the actors you would like to play certain parts, only to be told later that the part has already been cast with someone entirely different from the person you had in mind. On a series of your own creation, you may find that you get to work more closely with the producers.

When we wrote the radio show *Do Nothing 'Til You Hear From Me* (See Chapter 5), we were given a completely free hand as regards who we wanted to cast. As we were writing, we had certain actors' voices in our heads, with certain ways of delivering the lines, and luckily everyone we approached said yes. The cast list for our programme was like a who's who of British sitcom talent: Sam Kelly (*Porridge, 'Allo, 'Allo, On The Up, Cold Feet, Haggard, Barbara*), Melvyn Hayes (*It Ain't Half Hot Mum*), Caroline Lee Johnson (*Chef!*), Brian Bovell (*Gimme Gimme Gimme*) amongst others . . . oh, and some berk called Marcus Powell as well. As we have pointed out, to be given complete autonomy in this way is a very rare thing for a writer and so we grabbed the opportunity with both hands.

Recording in progress . . .

As a writer on a TV sitcom, your work is generally over by the time of an actual programme recording. At this point, your role becomes that of an audience member, albeit an audience member with extremely large butterflies in their stomach. A studio recording is a very exciting event, as it is, generally speaking, your only chance to see your script up and running.

Of course there have been the read throughs, and you may even have sat in on rehearsals, but you will suddenly find that there is a different dynamic to the actors' performances when in front of a live audience. This isn't to suggest that the actors haven't been giving their 'all' during the rehearsal, rather that the 'show' atmosphere gives their performances an added energy. When William G. Stewart was producer of the series *Bless This House*, he was quoted as saying that he noticed during an early rehearsal, that the star Sid James wasn't quite as animated as the producer would have liked. In a break, Stewart approached Sid, asking him about his apparent lethargy. Sid replied 'Bill, you've boxed a bit in your time, so you'll know what I mean – I never leave the fight in the gym'. And it was true. Actors generally rise to the occasion, and even those who have, up until then, given a relatively laid back reading, may still switch to 'level two' come the night. However, regardless of how prepared all concerned may be, accidents can still happen.

Hearing lines that you have written, being laughed at by a room full of complete strangers is an absolutely thrilling situation to be in. However, even the most polished of actors can occasionally make mistakes. Unlike the theatre, the actors on a TV show don't just carry on and try to extricate themselves from the situation, but rather they simply just stop and do it again. It could be a case of a forgotten line, or a malapropism. Equally, the reason for stopping could be purely technical, such as prop bottle not smashing as it did in rehearsals, or a coat tail getting stuck in the door. Whatever the reason, if you have any fingernails left by this point, prepare to bite down to your knuckles, as the actors have to go through the scene again, and the audience have to laugh uproariously at a joke they heard two minutes before. However good natured a studio audience may be (and they generally are – very), the law of diminishing returns is bound to come into play, but don't worry too much, because studio audiences usually consist of people who have been to a recording or two before, and as such, know a bit about the process. When asked by the producer or warm-up person to laugh at a joke they have already heard two or three times, they generally give it all they've got. The audience at a sitcom recording realise that they are a part of the show, and as such, want the evening to be as much of a success as you do. Of course, this is a generalisation, but it has been our experience that they will give their 'best' to a recording, provided of course that your show is any good to start with.

In radio, despite the fact that the actors are all reading directly from your script and as such do not have to 'learn' their lines, mistakes can still occur. However, if a line is fluffed, the actor simply pauses and then repeats the line almost immediately. In this way the scene maintains its momentum with little disturbance, unlike a scene on TV, which would have to be set up again from the beginning.

Depending on the size of the TV studio, your two or three main sets may be built side by side, and as such, allow the audience to view the scenes directly in front of them, as they would in a theatre. However, if your script involves any location filming, or studio scenes that for reasons of space couldn't be filmed on the night, these will be pre-filmed and played back on monitors, with the audience's reactions recorded. The episode will generally be recorded in one night, so this will be your only opportunity to see or hear your script being performed live. Victoria Wood recorded episodes of her series *dinnerladies* twice, allowing the cast to get a second stab at their roles and the producers the option of choosing the best response from the respective audiences. If a series has already been commissioned, then you can look forward to this exciting event several times over. However, if your script has only been commissioned as a pilot, this recording may be your only chance of seeing and hearing your characters and ideas come to life. If this is the case, don't be too downhearted. A successful pilot can stand you in good stead when next you come to pitch an idea for a new series. Using the video or audio recording of your pilot as a 'calling card' can open doors (or at least provide you with access to a meeting) far more easily than a writer with no 'back catalogue', even if your previous effort was never broadcast.

9. The Business of Being a Sitcom Writer

Throughout this book we've been making comparisons between American and UK sitcom styles – but this is definitely the chapter where the differences become even more obvious. As we've already mentioned, there's an existing television comedy industry in America which makes the prospect of forging a career in sitcom writing, if not a certainty, then at least a legitimate goal for the aspiring writer. Each TV season brings new sitcoms and teams of writers, some of which will go on to great things, some of which will fall by the wayside . . . but at least the industry is big and broad enough to give a lot of people their 'shot'.

On this side of the Atlantic the story is a little different. Yes, there are the 'big name' sitcom writers, from John Sullivan to Simon Nye, who can probably get new projects given serious consideration if not instant commissions on the strength of their names alone, and yes, the US system of team writing is being tried more and more over here, but the fact remains that the UK market is still a relatively small one with sitcoms vying for space in the schedules with (much cheaper to produce) 'reality' shows and quizzes.

It follows therefore that even if your aspirations are to spend your whole career turning out sitcoms, your best chance of gaining work and recognition in the UK comedy industry is to grab the chance to show off your comedy writing talents in whatever arena presents itself.

The comedy business, as with showbusiness in general, is as much about the business as it is about the show . . . and the best way to create a sustainable career for both you and your comic creations is to get the business side of your affairs sorted out as early as possible.

Whether you are already in a 'day job' or have no job at all, it is unlikely you will be given a staff writer's position – or even a trainee's job on an existing TV comedy right off the bat, so let's start from the assumption that just as you started your sitcom from a blank page back in the early chapters of this book, your comedy career is also a blank page. And just as with your writing, you need to lay some firm foundations careerwise before adding in all the clever ideas and interesting details.

Detail number one is to make a firm commitment to your writing. Collectively we've been writing comedy of one sort or another for over thirty years. And during that thirty years we've met lots of people both inside and outside showbusiness who tell us they have ambitions to write sitcoms, and that they could do as well or better than the writers whose work they see on the screen. We're sure they're right . . . unfortunately of these hundreds of people, neither of us can remember more than a handful who've gone beyond the talking stage and actually put pen to paper, not to mention the even smaller number who have kept at the writing through thick and thin. It will probably come as no surprise to discover that the writers we know who have ended up with material on the air have all been from that very small minority of people who spend less time talking about writing and more actually *writing*.

Rewarding though it can be when it all comes together, writing of any sort can also be a lonely frustrating business, and if you want the rewards, you also need to be ready for the hard slog . . . otherwise it's a bit like paying for a gym membership and never getting beyond the coffee bar. (We know, we've been there!)

If you HAVE made the commitment to write, then the first rule of business is to create the conditions where you can get as much value out of the time you put into writing as possible. A few screamingly basic principles can make all the difference in this regard, and first among these is finding a suitable place and time to write.

Whether you are fitting time in between a 9–5 job or have nothing to do all day but write, there is no 'right' set up that suits everyone. Some writers need complete silence and a carefully organised office, with full complement of modems, faxes and state-of-the-art PCs; others may settle themselves in a cafe or library, jotting down notes in longhand for transcribing later on. Writers with kids and not very much house space have been known to lock themselves in a bedroom or even the toilet for a snatched half hour of creativity. There is no ideal time to write either – John tends to get up around 3 or 4am and write until late morning when the phones start to hop and concentration becomes impossible. Marcus on the other hand is a night owl, often working through the night on scripts and treatments . . . we often joke that most of our collaborations have to be fitted into the two hour window when we're both awake. Joking aside, getting a good idea of how your own bodyclock operates in relation to writing can be a great help when you're writing to deadline – especially if you can organise your time to be writing in the hours when your energy and productivity is the highest.

Whatever time you write best, try to develop the discipline of writing at the same time every day – just like your physical muscles (and ours, when we're not in the coffee bar) your mental and creative muscles are developed through constantly exercising them. At the beginning of your comedy writing career you may have few or no actual deadlines to meet, but trust us, getting into a habit of writing regularly will pay dividends when the pressure is on and you're only as good as your last script (a script that the producer usually wants yesterday!)

It's the point when you don't have any deadlines which often marks the difference between a real writer and a 'wannabe'. Almost any of us can get ourselves motivated to write when there's a producer waiting at the other end of the fax and the prospect of a commission or fame and fortune – yet it's the motivation to write for no other reason than to hone our skills that will eventually bring those commissions and opportunities knocking on our door.

Close relation to the 'no time' excuse for not taking the plunge into a serious comedy writing career is the 'no money' stronghold. This manifests in two ways. The first group of patients tends to give excuses along the lines of 'Yes, I'd love to concentrate on my writing more, but in the meantime I've got to work to pay the rent.' As we've already noted above, writing of any sort demands commitment and even sacrifice . . . or at the very least making choices. Yes, we know you've got to work to make a living but if you're still finding time to fit in socialising, your Saturday football game or a slouch on the sofa in front of your favourite soap, you may want to ask yourself if you can find some time from these activities which might be more usefully employed in the service of your comedy career . . . or perhaps just acknowledge that in your list of priorities, dreaming about writing is more important then actually doing it.

Lest we sound too harsh, let's quickly point out that many of the aspiring writers we know make great sacrifices to pursue their careers – sometimes to an extent we wouldn't necessarily encourage. For instance, if you're ploughing away at your sitcom script confident that it is the next *Friends* or *Mr Bean* and that once the world acknowledges its greatness you'll be able to take your huge advance cheque and deal with the large pile of brown envelopes that's building up on your welcome mat, well can we suggest you stop and take a look at things from a more realistic perspective. You'll note that we're not suggesting your sitcom isn't the next global mega hit – hey, you've got this wonderful book on your side, haven't you? It's just that we've seen a lot of writers, not to mention actors, comics and musicians slip into serious debt by putting all their eggs in one basket and waiting for the 'big break' to pull their fat out of the fire.

The truth is that it's very difficult to be funny or maintain any kind of perspective on your writing if you're increasingly hungry, stressed and in desperate need of a commission to sort out your financial woes. Not only that, but too close a focus on writing to the exclusion of the outside world is particularly bad news for sitcom projects – after all, you're aiming to create real situations and characters who appeal to real people, and cutting yourself off from real people in your writer's garret isn't the best way to achieve that.

Even if you DO land the big project, the previous chapters should forewarn you that it can be quite a long journey from having interest shown in a script, through developing it and rewriting several times to getting it recorded . . . and an even longer journey before serious amounts of cash actually end up in your hands. Sure, £2–3000 sounds like a lot of money for a pilot script when you see a commission reported in the broadcast press – but bear in mind that that's often the only money the writer will see for a year or more. Divided by twelve months it's not an awful lot of money to live on by anyone's standards.

The good news is that not only is it perfectly possible to find part-time or full-time work which will sustain your writing activities, but the experience gained in the real world can give you lots of inspiration for your creative endeavours. Being able to afford decent working materials and keeping your electricity on is a big boost to creativity too.

If you're not already in a full-time job and have your sitcom idea set in a particular work environment, you could always try and take on some part-time work in the same area to help the creative juices flow . . . if nothing else, it will make a great story for chat shows after you win your comedy award. Joking aside though, being conscious of your own writing patterns and 'bodyclock' will help you choose a job that suits – if you're a morning writer you may want to keep that time free to turn out your masterpiece, and find a part-time job later in the day to pay the rent. On the other hand a 'day job' can work very well as long as you can sustain the energy to hit the typewriter afterwards when everyone else is either heading out to socialise or flopping into bed.

One point to bear in mind is that many undiscovered scriptwriters and novelists gravitate towards jobs which involve writing – such as copywriting, editing or journalism – on the grounds that while it's not quite the kind of writing they actually want to do, it's a close cousin and keeps them in practise. This approach can work very well for many people – however, you may also need to ask yourself if, having spent all the working day plugging away at a keyboard, you're going to be particularly keen to do more writing on your time off. A similar wheeze is to get a job in some other branch of the entertainment industry whether as a receptionist, a runner or a secretary, on the grounds that it's a good way to build up contacts and insider knowledge. It can certainly work: *Fools and Horses* writer John Sullivan famously sold his first sitcom after bumping into a TV executive in the bar while he was working as a scene shifter.

These days, though, the media world has got so corporate that if you accost executives in the bar the only 'hit' you are likely to end up with is from the security guard . . . and the point of John Sullivan's story is that before he had his 'lucky break' he put the time and effort into actually having a good script to talk about in the first place.

Sitcom industry or no sitcom industry, you can of course decide to polish your comic skills and even earn some extra cash in the more general field of comedy writing. From stand-up to sketch shows to the Internet, there are always new markets opening up if you are prepared to put the effort into finding them. (How you go about finding them is a little outside the scope of this particular book . . . but very much in the scope of *Writing Comedy*, John's previous book in the same series as this one.)

Before closing the discussion about money, it's worth saying a word about tax (and no, it's not one of the words the publishers won't let us use in this book). The bad news is that any income you make from your sitcom or other comedy writing activities is taxable, over and above any tax you are already paying on other full-time or part-time jobs. Indeed if you're not registered for tax, a lot of the larger broadcasters and production companies will have difficulty paying you. The good news is that once you do register for tax, a lot of your comedy expenditure, from stationery supplies to videos and DVDs, may be claimed as legitimate expenses.

Contact your local tax office for details of how to register and information on when your returns are due. (They charge a hefty fee for late returns which isn't funny at all.)

With all the struggles and sacrifices inherent in working as a freelance scriptwriter, it's not surprising that so many comedy writers gravitate towards working in teams. Many of the great sitcoms we've referred to elsewhere in the book have been produced by writing teams, usually couples and there's no question that names like Galton and Simpson, Muir and Norden, or Clement and La Frenais seem as intrinsically linked behind the comedy scenes as Laurel and Hardy, and Morecambe and Wise were in front of the cameras. However, like any other kind of successful couple, creating a successful sitcom pairing can be a process of trial and error. It's worth choosing your partner wisely – after all you may end up spending more time together than the average married couple.

Comedy writing teams can grow out of chance meetings in writing courses, writers' rooms in TV companies or by proactively advertising for a partner in a broadcast or literary magazine. If you feel a partnership would be a step forward for you, we can pretty much guarantee that there are several other writers out there somewhere in exactly the same boat, and finding one of them won't be all that difficult with a little effort and detective work. But getting the right person and learning to work together so you both steer the boat in the right direction can be a slightly harder task.

Both Marcus and John have had the experience of working as a team, working as individuals and working on projects with other writers. Our preference? Well, in all honesty we don't have one. Working as a team, particularly with someone you like, can be a lot more fun – you can laugh at each other's jokes, bounce ideas off each other, and have someone to moan to on the days when the jokes don't flow and the producer phones up demanding a fifth rewrite.

Inevitably, working as a partnership also brings its fair share of compromise – not every joke you want to put in is going to get your partner's approval and vice versa. Being able to argue for what you think works best without getting the hump if your partner has a better idea is possibly an even more important skill in team writing than your comedy writing abilities themselves.

It's also true that while you may enjoy spending time in the company of a like-minded soul, you may get more work done if you team up with someone whose skills are a little different to yours. In many successful teams one writer is strong on plot or character, while the other may be better at gags. One writer may be the one who does most of the typing while the other one stares out of the window and calls out ideas. Equally we know writing teams where both writers sit at the keyboard and argue over each line before it goes on the page.

As we've said before there are no 'right ways', only ways that work. When we write something together we tend to have an initial discussion, say to work out the characters and scene breakdown if we're working on a sitcom, then divide the work up into more or less equal chunks. One of us may take the first half of the show and write all the scenes ourselves while the other works on the ending. Then we swap over with each of us editing the other's work. Interestingly, even though we both have different strengths, working in this way means the end product is not only stronger than each of us could have achieved individually, it's often hard for the reader who hasn't been party to the writing process to work out which bits Marcus wrote and which bits John wrote in the finished script. In all honesty, we often can't remember either.

That last factor is probably the key one in forging a successful writing partnership. Creativity by its nature often involves ego and if both partners can't get their egos to work in tandem, the writing team is likely to be extremely short lived. We've already noted that different writers have different ways of working and while your way of working doesn't have to be identical to your partner's, it certainly has to complement it. For instance, simple issues like time-keeping can cause problems – if one partner is a stickler for deadlines and the other is more laid back, friction can quickly arise. This can particularly be the case if one partner has a lot of other commitments such as parenting and family duties while the other is footloose and fancy free.

On the other hand, two single people involved in a writing project may find that the intensity and intimacy that is a necessary part of creating something together spills into more personal areas. Even if there's no hanky panky involved, if you have already got a life partner you may well have some difficulty explaining why you're suddenly spending more time with your writing partner than you are with them.

With all these considerations in mind, it's obviously best to use one particular project to 'test drive' a particular writing partnership and see if it works for both of you, before making it a more permanent arrangement. Even if it does work it's probably best for each writer to keep working on independent projects too. Not only will this mean each writer is bringing fresh inspiration and contacts to the team, it also avoids the phenomenon which Jurgen Wolff so astutely comments on in his own sitcom writing book: when a comedy writing team breaks up for whatever reason, people always assume the *other* writer was the funny one.

Just as comedy writing teams can come into being for a variety of reasons, they can come to an end because of a variety of factors too. Obviously, creative and personal differences can lead to acrimony – but pairings can come to a natural end too. It may simply be that as both writers develop their own abilities their goals change – for instance, one may wish to continue working in the sitcom field, the other may want to turn their hand to writing screenplays or even the great novel. Despite what the old song says, if the team hasn't as yet had huge success then breaking up shouldn't really be all that hard to do.

On the other hand, comedy history is full of stories of famous and successful pairs who were forced to keep working together even though they actually hated each other because they were linked together in the public mind. This phenomenon is much more common onstage than behind the scenes, but the subject of break ups and their ramifications is as good a point as any to bring up that most businesslike aspect of the sitcom business: contracts, copyright and other legal agreements.

While it's relatively easy to get even the most disorganised comedy writer to see the benefits of better financial and time management, talking about legal stuff is almost guaranteed to get the average comic brain to switch off – which is exactly why the legal side of comedy writing causes such grief for all concerned. At the team writing level, it can seem very crass to introduce the idea of an agreement early on in what is basically a meeting of minds and a relationship based on mutual respect . . . yet the beginning of the relationship is EXACTLY the time to put on paper what both writing partners want and expect from the collaboration and each other. It doesn't need to be a formal contract – a simple exchange of personal letters will do fine, but trust us, getting things clear when there's no money on the table is a very good way of heading off the rows, ill feeling and bruised egos that often eat away at comedy teams as soon as money and deadline pressure do become part of the picture. By the way, any agreement with your writing partner also needs to look at areas such as how credits and rights to material are split. For instance, how is your joint work to be credited? Alphabetically? And what happens if both partners work on an idea that was originally thought of by one of you rather than in a brainstorming session, or based around an existing character that one of the writers developed before the partnership began? A properly thought out writing agreement may be a bit of a pain now, but it saves a lot more pain later on.

For what it's worth, we ourselves tend to alternate our writing credits, so that one script or series is credited 'Marcus Powell and John Byrne' and the next 'John Byrne and Marcus Powell'. We've forgotten whether this was a conscious decision or whether one of us thought it up, but it certainly works for us. We split royalties from any joint project fifty-fifty regardless of who originally thought it up – it makes life easier in the long run, particularly since neither of us is a big fan of maths.

Whether you are a single writer or part of a team, the real test comes when interest is shown in one of your projects and you get offered an option or commission contract. How do you pass the test? By *not* taking it on – get qualified legal advice before you sign any documents. There are enough horror stories out there to show this is good common sense advice, but it's a lot harder to follow when after weeks and maybe months of slogging away on your script and career with no comeback and possibly not much food either, there's suddenly a large advance payment in prospect, and you're being wined and dined by a TV company and invited to suggest which of your favourite stars you think should be cast in your sitcom's lead role.

However, if you really do care about your sitcom this is exactly when you should start getting cautious about exactly what rights you are signing away.

While companies may talk about 'standard contracts' it's best to work on the assumption that every contract is different. We're not suggesting for a minute that you work from the assumption that everybody you meet is out to shaft you – writers with 'attitude' are not very attractive to serious employers – at the same time don't forget that any contracts produced by a broadcaster or a production company's legal department are primarily designed to protect *their* interests. You are perfectly entitled to question clauses you don't like and negotiate a deal that better suits you – but that's where getting good legal advice comes in.

We're definitely not claiming to be legal experts, but here are some of the things which tend to come in standard contracts which you and your advisors may want to consider:

Contract details

Payment

Yes, we know it's not the principal motivation of every sitcom writer, but you have certainly worked hard enough to get to the stage when an offer is on the table, so you are entitled to be recompensed properly. As we've already noted, it can be hard to turn down a 'big' advance if money is tight, but if you really believe in your work it may be worth checking with your advisors to see if you can keep a percentage of the project's ownership too. After all, it may be nice to have a couple of thousand in your pocket right now, but what if the show goes on to become a huge worldwide hit and you get nothing from the international sales, merchandise and the movie spin-off?

Normally an advance payment is split into an immediate sum when you sign the contract, a further amount when the first draft is accepted and a final payment, often on the first day of shooting.

Check whether you're being asked to write an individual script or a series under the same agreement . . . and make sure it's possible to do so timewise as there can be penalties for late delivery.

Rewrites and copyright

Just as you should take a close look at the money situation in any contract you are offered, you should also be very clear on exactly what rights you are signing away when you put pen to paper. Yes, the production company or TV are putting their investment into fleshing out your script and ideas and they are entitled to ask for rewrites and polishing to get the best possible script for their investment. On the other hand, you are entitled to know how many rewrites you will be expected to do before you can start charging extra. You also need to know how a decision will be reached on what constitutes an acceptable script. There are several sad stories we know where writers have signed away their ownership and been removed from their own projects.

On a happier note, if the show does become a hit and gets commissioned for another, longer series, you may not want to write the whole lot yourself. If there are other writers and teams brought in to work on your 'baby' you'll probably still want to have a degree of control over what they're writing, and you'll certainly be looking to get some money even if you're not writing the show. After all, nobody else would be making money if it wasn't for your original ideas.

Formats and merchandising rights

Almost everybody who has ever worked for a living will agree that the best kind of work is the sort that goes on earning after the initial job has been done. Don't skim over clauses about formats and merchandising rights too quickly . . . they are often more relevant to your future income than the clauses relating to the original writing job. Established teams like Chesney and Wolfe have not only earned income from countless re-runs of hit sitcoms like *On The Buses* and *The Rag Trade*, they have also had the pleasure of seeing the basic series concept and scripts sold to other countries and then adapted into a local format with local performers and culturally relevant jokes and settings. Often the original writers get to oversee the new project and are well paid to do so.

As for merchandising rights, well, from *Red Dwarf* to *The Simpsons*, the potential earnings from T-shirts, mugs, DVDS and action figures often mount up to far more than any income from the script itself. Sorry to be boring about this, but get that legal advice and be wary of what you are signing away.

Comedy meets computers

Legal moans and cautionary tales aside, it will hopefully be clear from the pages that have gone before, that we have a healthy respect for the great tradition of sitcom on both sides of the Atlantic. On the other hand, like any art form, sitcom will only stay alive if it adapts to changing times and that means sitcom writers having to adapt also. It certainly pays for any serious writer to have at least a basic knowledge of the various bits of technology which make the whole writing process easier – from script writing programs like 'Final Draft' which format and lay out scripts for you in approved format (there are even special sitcom add-ons) to the vast number of writing resources which are available on the Internet. There are even packages like 'Blockbuster' and 'Story Craft' which claim to help with the creative as well as the practical art of writing, coming up with plots and even gags on demand.

If you are part of a writing team it may be that one of you is the tech and the other is more ludic, but you will both certainly find that you are increasingly asked to submit scripts and amendments via e-mail or other electronic means, so if you are a lone scribe who doesn't know a PC from a VCR, it's certainly worth persuading a technically minded friend to act as your computer guru.

151

Many enterprising writers have even set up their own websites and who is to say commissions won't increasingly come their way through this medium? More to the point, with the advent of broadband technology it is perfectly possible that online sitcoms may be a phenomenon of the future – there have been some interesting experiments in this area already.

Not only will that cut out the whole pesky business of selling yourself to individual production companies and networks, you will be able to produce your own niche market sitcoms and promote them directly to your target audience. So there may well be hope for all those ideas you discarded back in the early chapters which you really loved but felt there would never be a wide enough audience for!

It's up to you . . .

Well, obviously we hope your career is filled with more and more sitcom hits of ever increasing success. Maybe you'll even employ us on your writing team when you're in your fifth series and the workload is just too much for you to manage. Equally, if all you've managed to do is put your first script together with the help of this book we're just as proud of you. What you do with it now, though, makes the difference between being a sitcom writer and being in the sitcom writing business – if you're happy to rest on your laurels, well we're happy to celebrate right along with you. But if your script is already in the mail to several production companies and you're hard at work on sitcom project number two, then you're well on the way to developing the perseverance and commitment that combined with your writing talents will give you the best possible chance of getting your show on the air and your career off the ground. If you need some further guidance along the way, feel free to contact us at marcus&john@webtoonist.com – even more so if you've picked up any further hints and tips we haven't included here. After all, we sincerely hope that when it comes to writing the second edition of this book, one of the classic sitcoms we'll be encouraging readers to study will be yours!

10. The Sitcom Writers

Over the years there have been many sitcoms which have entertained, enthralled, occasionally annoyed, but (if you are a sitcom writer yourself) mostly inspired us. From early practitioners of the art such as Muir and Norden, Galton and Simpson, and Richard Waring in the 1950s and 60s, through names such as Cooke and Mortimer and Carla Lane in the 1970s, right up to contemporary sitcom writers such as Ben Elton and Simon Nye, regardless of the show's undoubted success or relative failure, it has all started from the written word. There are many writers who have proven themselves successful in other areas of comedy writing, venturing into sitcom territory perhaps only once or twice in their careers (John Cleese and Connie Booth with *Fawlty Towers* for example), whereas others have stuck firmly to the situation comedy form, notching up series after series (Roy Clarke, to name but one). Many writers have used the genre to tackle certain themes in different settings: Johnny Speight's handling of the issues of race relations in *Till Death Us Do Part* and *Curry and Chips*; Carla Lane's explorations of female independence in *The Liver Birds*, *Solo* and *Screaming*; David Croft and Jimmy Perry's hymns to nostalgia and the group dynamic in *Dad's Army*, *It Ain't Half Hot Mum* and *Hi-De-Hi*.

In this chapter is a list of some of the writers who have made a major contribution to the art of British TV sitcom writing, as well as their credits. Our criteria for inclusion was any UK writer(s) (with one notable exception) with four or more different series under their belts, and/or for the sheer longevity of their respective creations. We do not claim that this is a list of the best writers (that is not for us to judge, although in certain instances this may well be the case), merely a selection of some of the most prolific. You may find that we have failed to include some of the more obvious names, and, in truth, there are certain writers who have notched up an impressive list of credits but have not been included simply because of space. If you consider how many sitcoms have been produced in the UK alone in the past 50 years, to list all the writers involved would take up all the pages of a whole other book (who knows, perhaps we may tackle it yet). For the purposes of this list, however, we have whittled the choices down to ten in alphabetical order, spanning the 1950s to the present. Amongst the titles, we are sure you will find many series that are rightly regarded as classics, as well as some obscurities. Some may be completely new to you, while others will serve as a pleasant memory jog. Whatever the case, we hope you take the time to seek out some of these series (some may be playing on Cable, if not terrestrial TV as we speak, while others will be readily available on video and DVD), and while some may be 'of their time', others are as funny today as when they were originally broadcast.

Eric Chappell

Perhaps best known for writing *Rising Damp*, Chappell has notched up an amazing list of ITV sitcom credits. In 1974 Chappell created and wrote the pilot episode for the office sitcom *The Squirrels*, which went on to run for three series from 1975 to 1978. Simultaneously, he adapted his stage play *The Banana Box*, about life in a small town boarding house, turning it into *Rising Damp*, a runaway success which itself ran for four series from 1974 to 1978, as well as spawning a big screen version in 1980. Not one to rest on his hands or his laurels, Chappell followed *Rising Damp* with such series as the hospital set *Only When I Laugh* (1979–1982), *The Bounder* (1982–83) and three series of the Spanish hotel set comedy *Duty Free* (1984–86) in collaboration with Jean Warr. More recent series have included *Haggard* (1990–92), the adventures of an 18th century squire and his companions, and a return to the office setting with *Fiddlers Three* (1991).

Roy Clarke

At the time of writing, Roy Clarke's most successful series (certainly the longest running) *Last of the Summer Wine* has been on air for 30 years. As the sole writer of well over 150 half hours (not to mention numerous 'extended' specials) of this gentle, yet consistently amusing series, his place in the annals of sitcom history would certainly be assured, but what is even more remarkable is the fact that during that time, he has also created and written such other hit series as *Open All Hours* (four series from 1976–1985), and *Keeping Up Appearances* (five series from 1990–1995). As if all this were not enough, Clarke has found time to write several other series during this period, including *Potter* (three series, 1979–83) following the adventures of a pompous, retired company chairman Redvers Potter, *Rosie* (five series, 1977–78) about a young police officer (Clarke himself served a stint in the police force, as well as being a teacher before turning to a scriptwriting career), and *The Magnificent Evans* (1984) featuring Ronnie Barker as the Welsh photographer Plantagenet Evans. In addition to the ongoing *Summer Wine*, Clarke's most recent series was *Spark* (1997), about a man in early middle age who finally gets a chance to sample life following the death of his overbearing mother. All in all, Roy Clarke has probably written over 400 episodes of some 14 different sitcom series, not to mention one-off sitcoms, such as his *Spanners Eleven* episode in Ronnie Barker's *Seven Of One* series (1973) and several dramatic scripts prior to his sitcom career. Apparently 'Eating' and 'Sleeping' are next on his 'Things to do' list.

Dick Clement and Ian La Frenais

In the 1960s, Clement and La Frenais' more 'naturalistic' approach to sitcom writing paid off huge dividends with the success of their series *The Likely Lads*, following the exploits of two young working class friends, Terry and Bob, in the North East of England, which ran for three series over three years (1964–66). In 1973 the writers returned to catch up with the continuing tale of the 'Lads', creating an even more successful series: *Whatever Happened To The Likely Lads . . . ?* This ran for two series of 27 episodes from 1973–74, before spinning off into a big screen version in 1976. After the initial run of *The Likely Lads*, Clement and La Frenais found themselves in very auspicious company, when they wrote the majority of episodes for a short lived series entitled *Mr Aitch* starring Harry 'H' Corbett (Galton and Simpson also wrote several episodes) in

1967. That same year they wrote a sitcom based on Kingsley Amis' novel *Lucky Jim*, depicting university life in the Swinging Sixties. The writers returned to the character and subject in 1982 with *The Further Adventures of . . .* However, their crowning glory was arguably still to come. In 1974 they looked at the exploits of two small-time criminals in the series *Thick As Thieves*, before following a life of crime to its inevitable conclusion with their prison set smash hit series *Porridge*. Starting with the pilot episode in 1973, to the final 'lights out' in 1977, *Porridge* became almost a masterclass in British sitcom writing and performance. So successful was Clement and La Frenais' creation, that the series spawned not only a feature film version but a sequel as well: *Going Straight* featured the central *Porridge* characters Fletcher and Godber adapting to life on the outside, but as a series it was sadly short-lived. Most recently, the writers have been working on the big screen, writing the screenplays for, amongst others, *The Commitments* and *Still Crazy*.

David Croft/Jimmy Perry/Jeremy Lloyd

As a producer and writer, in collaboration with both Jimmy Perry and Jeremy Lloyd respectively, David Croft has been responsible for some of the most popular BBC sitcoms of the past 35 years. His partnership with Jimmy Perry produced not only nine series of the classic *Dad's Army* from 1968–1977, (as well as a feature film and a stage musical version) but also that other wartime comedy *It Ain't Half Hot Mum*, which itself ran for eight series between 1974 and 1981. Following the continuing success of both these series, Croft and Perry turned their attentions to the decade immediately after the war and a setting where people's minds were fixed firmly on fun – the holiday camp. *Hi-De-Hi!* began its run in 1980, continuing for 58 episodes over the next eight years. *You Rang, M'Lord?* started almost immediately following the end of *Hi-De-Hi!*, utilising the talents of many actors from the writers' previous series, running for four series until 1993. However, despite the undoubted popularity of these other shows, *Dad's Army* remains the jewel in the Croft and Perry crown.

Croft's collaboration with Jeremy Lloyd was no less prolific, producing ten series of *Are You Being Served?* from the pilot in 1972 to the final episode in 1985 (a full length feature film was also made in 1977, as well as a stage version). Croft returned with Lloyd to another wartime comedy, this time set in occupied France – the phenomenally successful *'Allo 'Allo* (85 episodes from 1982–1992) which itself spawned a hit stage version.

Ben Elton

Along with Rik Mayall and Lise Mayer, Ben Elton co-wrote the first 'alternative' sitcom *The Young Ones* back in 1982, about a quartet of anarchic students sharing a flat. For two riotously unpredictable series, Elton and his fellow writers twisted, turned and tickled the traditional sitcom format until it was left gasping and dizzy. Treading a similarly surreal path as *The Young Ones* (albeit with less of the slapstick violence), Elton's first solo written sitcom *Happy Families* came in 1985 for one series. The following year he was to team up with Richard Curtis on the second series of *Blackadder*. The previous series had been written by Curtis with the series' star Rowan Atkinson, but had proven to be less successful than all concerned would have hoped. Atkinson decided to forego writing duties on the second series, but with the introduction of Elton to the team, however, things took a definite turn for the better. Out went the location filming and slightly dim persona of the original Blackadder, to be replaced by unashamedly studio bound settings, a smoother, more wily Blackadder delivering razor sharp deliciously convoluted one-liners, and no small measure of cartoon violence. The Elton/Curtis team was to prove the winning formula, taking the series through a further 18 episodes and three specials over the next three years. Elton's most recent attempt at a solo written series, *The Thin Blue Line*, reunited him with Rowan Atkinson, but in a far less anarchic and more traditional feeling sitcom. Elton's admiration for Croft and Perry's *Dad's Army* is apparent in the warm ensemble playing of this police station set comedy which ran for two series from 1995–1996.

John Esmonde and Bob Larbey

Esmonde and Larbey's first foray into TV sitcom writing came in 1966 when they wrote a series entitled *Room at the Bottom* about the boiler room activities of a group of crafty maintenance workers, but their first real success came in 1968 with the creation of the popular classroom comedy *Please Sir!* This ran for four series until 1972 (a spin-off feature film was released in 1971), eventually spawning the spin-off series *The Fenn Street Gang*, which followed the exploits of the pupils once they had left school. This again proved massively popular, lasting three series from 1971–73. As if this wasn't enough, Esmonde and Larbey then ventured on another spin-off (this time following a supporting character from the Fenn Street Gang, 'Mr. Bowler'), but *Bowler* (13 episodes in 1973) was to prove the least successful of the three series. Esmonde and Larbey moved on to arguably even greater success when they wrote the delightful self-sufficiency comedy *The Good Life*, which ran for four series between 1975 and 1978. Simultaneously, the duo wrote *Get Some In!* about a group of National Servicemen in the late 1950s. This ran for five series during the same 1975–78 period.

Bob Larbey went on to write solo series such as *A Fine Romance* (four series, 1981–84) and the hugely popular *As Time Goes By*, which from 1992–2002 has gone on to provoke a fiercely loyal following, both nationally and overseas. Larbey's most recent solo series was *My Good Friend* starring George Cole, which followed the newly formed relationship between two elderly men, and ran for two series from 1995–96.

Ray Galton and Alan Simpson
Arguably the most revered of British sitcom writers, Galton and Simpson began writing sketch and stand-up material for radio shows such as *Happy Go Lucky* and *Star Bill* in the early 1950s. In 1954, having written various sketches for him on both stage and radio, the duo teamed up with Tony Hancock, creating the classic *Hancock's Half Hour*. This justly celebrated series ran on radio for six series until 1959, following as it did, the exploits of Hancock, Sid James and Bill Kerr. The series switched to TV in 1956, itself running for five years and seven series – the last series being entitled simply *Hancock*, and featuring Tony Hancock without his usual co-star Sid James. This last series is the one Galton and Simpson are probably most famous for, containing as it does, classic episodes such as 'The Bedsitter' and 'The Blood Donor', to name but two. Following the break up of the Galton/Simpson/Hancock/James partnerships, Galton and

Simpson were approached to write a series exclusively for Sid James. The result was *Citizen James*, following the adventures of a crafty cockney, not unlike James' character in the Hancock series. The series ran for three seasons from 1960–62, although Galton and Simpson contributed solely to the first series of six episodes (the second and third series were written by another celebrated partnership Sid Green and Dick Hills, who enjoyed success as Morecambe and Wise's scriptwriters on their early BBC series). In 1961 Galton and Simpson wrote two series of one-off half hour comedies under the banner *Comedy Playhouse* (subsequent series under this title were written by a variety of writers). Of the 16 programmes the team wrote for the first two series, one would go on to become a bona fide classic. *The Offer*, first broadcast on 5th January 1962, explored the father and son relationship of a pair of rag and bone men. The BBC decided to turn this one-off show into a series, and so *Steptoe and Son* was born. Running for 59 episodes from 1962–1974 (including two feature film spin-offs), Steptoe is widely regarded as one of the finest sitcoms ever produced. The 1970s saw the duo writing several other series under the *Playhouse* banner, as well as series such as *Casanova '73* starring Leslie Philips, and (Les) *Dawson's Weekly* in 1975.

In 1979 Ray Galton teamed up with Johnny Speight to write three series of the police comedy *Spooner's Patch* (1979–82). Most recently Galton has partnered John Antrobus on such series as *Room at the Bottom* (two series from 1986–88) an 80s adaptation of Antrobus' 1964 series about the inner workings of a TV company, and *Get Well Soon* (one series – 1997), the 1940s set comedy about life in a TB sanatorium (the location of Galton and Simpson's first meeting in 1947).

Larry Gelbart

Larry Gelbart's career has spanned six decades, starting at the tender age of 16 as a staff writer for Maxwell House Coffee Hour, before writing for such legendary comedians as Bob Hope and Eddie Cantor, as well as sketches for UK comedians such as Dick Emery and Marty Feldman. Gelbart wrote alongside such luminaries as Neil Simon, Carl Reiner and Mel Brooks for Sid Caesar on his *Your Show Of Shows* TV show, one of the most famous of the 1950s, as well as working with

Woody Allen on Caesar's TV specials. Gelbart moved into writing for the theatre with such hit shows as the Tony Award winning *A Funny Thing Happened On The Way To The Forum* and *City of Angels*. In 1972 Larry Gelbart created (with Gene Reynolds) the TV version of the popular film *M*A*S*H*. This smash hit sitcom was to run for 251 episodes over 11 years, with Gelbart as one of the main writers. The series was to go on to win 14 Emmy Awards, and 109 nominations in total, as well as Peabody and Humanitas Awards. The final episode broadcast on 28th February 1983, was seen by 125 million Americans, the highest viewing figure ever at that time. In the early 80s Gelbart wrote 13 episodes of a thought-provoking sitcom *United States*, which dealt with many adult themes, breaking many sitcom conventions in the process. More recently Gelbart has been scriptwriter on such feature films as *Tootsie* and *Oh God* starring George Burns.

Carla Lane

Without doubt, Carla Lane is the most prolific writer in an industry where women are still grossly under represented. In recent years Jennifer Saunders and Caroline Aherne have contributed greatly to the genre with popular series such as *Absolutely Fabulous* and *The Royle Family*, but they both have a long way to go to equal Lane's impressive tally of over a dozen different series to date. In 1969 Lane and her then partner Myra Taylor created *The Liver Birds*, following the exploits of a pair of single woman in Liverpool. This hugely popular series ran for nine series from 1969–79, with a tenth series revival in 1996. During the writing of the early series of *The Liver Birds*, Lane and Taylor also contributed 15 episodes of *Bless This House*, with Lane going on to write a further ten as a solo writer. In 1974 *No Strings*, Lane's contribution to the *Comedy Playhouse* series, became a series in its own right, running for seven episodes, before she had another huge success with *Butterflies*, an incredibly popular series which ran for four seasons from 1978–1983. Many of Lane's successive series dealt with non-typical sitcom themes such as adultery from the point of view of the 'other woman' (*The Mistress* – two series 1985–87) and alcoholism (*I Woke Up Screaming* – two series 1985–86). 1986 saw the creation of *Bread*, focusing on life with the Boswell family. This popular series ran for 74 episodes between 1986-1991, and despite the fact that Ms Lane has written several series since, it has yet to be rivaled for longevity (*The Liver Birds* notwithstanding).

John Sullivan

If viewing figures are anything to go by, John Sullivan is probably the most popular British sitcom writer of the past twenty years. Prior to his career as a writer, he had been, amongst other things, a market trader (which was to prove invaluable when researching for his most popular series) and a BBC studio worker (which put him in an ideal position to have his initial script seen.) His first series *Citizen Smith* centred on the activities of South London militant Wolfie Smith, leader of the Tooting Popular Front. This hugely enjoyable, and fondly remembered series ran for 30 episodes between 1977–80. Sticking to his South London locations and drawing on his days in the market, Sullivan followed the success of *Citizen Smith* with *Only Fools and Horses*. This story of the Trotter brothers and their attempts to make it out of their Peckham tower block and into the big time, has gone on to become the most successful British sitcom of all time. Since 1981, the adventures of Del and Rodney have delighted millions. In the case of the final episode of series 8, 24.35 million viewers tuned in.

While working on the third series of 'Fools', Sullivan created another, *Just Good Friends*. This was the story of Vince and Penny, formerly engaged to be married, who meet up again several years later and rekindle their relationship. This hilarious series ran for 22 episodes from 1983–86, and bore all the Sullivan hallmarks of earthy characterization and witty, razor sharp dialogue. These traits were on ample display with Sullivan's next series, the brilliant *Dear John*, which sadly ran for only two series in 1986–87. The concept was sold to US TV, with several of the episodes being written by Sullivan himself, and ran for 90 episodes, however only 32 of the US version were ever broadcast on UK TV. Most recently, Sullivan has created *Roger Roger*, (pilot episode broadcast 1996) a sitcom set in the world of cab drivers, which at the time of writing is due to start a new series.

11. Resource Section

We'll start with a quote: 'No man is an island'. Well, for that matter, 'No man is a carrier bag or a packet of digestive biscuits!' but let's stick with the first quote for the time being.

In the same way you would not be expected to compose music without ever having heard or read another composer's work, or make a piece of furniture without ever looking at the way a table or chair is constructed, it makes sense that in order to write a script, good, bad or indifferent, you have to read other writers' work.

There are many books on the market about writing: some specifically to do with comedy, while others are more general. There are even a few that deal with the subject of sitcoms (well, you're holding one for a start). However, it may not hurt to read a few of the books that deal more generally with writing techniques, dramatic structure, etc. If you are a first-time writer, regardless of your preferred genre these types of books will give you an overview of how to express your ideas on paper.

Aside from the books on technique, there are, of course, many books of actual scripts available. From classic shows to more contemporary offerings, it seems that all genres have their literary tie-ins, and a good thing too. Reading the work of say, Richard Curtis and Ben Elton or Marta Kauffman and David Crane (the creators of *Friends*), will give you a much better idea of how to structure your dialogue, plots and dovetailing subplots etc, laid out on the page, than when you are actually watching an episode of their respective series.

If you go into any of the larger High Street music shops, you are bound to find hundreds of comedy programmes on video and DVD. Equally, if you look in the spoken word section of most bookshops, you will find various examples of the BBC's radio output, as well as US offerings of classic shows from the likes of Burns and Allen, and Jack Benny.

You may also feel inspired to browse in second-hand record shops. It's amazing the recordings you can discover, preserved on vinyl and long since deleted. In the past it has been our pleasure to uncover gems such as specially re-recorded versions of Galton and Simpson's 'The Blood Donor' and 'The Radio Ham' on a long forgotten 33rpm. (*For the younger readers, 33rpm is a bit like a big black CD.*)

You may prefer to surf the net for your information. This is, of course, entirely up to you. The Internet is an absolutely marvellous resource for sitcom writers, allowing you the opportunity to download transcribed copies of scripts, information on and images of obscure series and performers, credits and biographies of writers, as well as practical advice on the craft of sitcom writing.

Below is a list of books, organisations and websites that we have found useful. You may find that they are of no use to *you* whatsoever. If so, that would be a great shame, but this is by no means a comprehensive list, and it may simply be that the material that will prove most inspirational and/or instructive to you is waiting just around the corner. In the meantime, however, indulge us, and check out some of these titles.

Books

Writing Dialogue Tom Chiarella (Story Press, 1998)

Tom Chiarella is a US university English lecturer as well as an author, and while not pertaining specifically to comic dialogue, and actually aimed at the budding novelist, this is an excellent, informative and very accessible book. As the cover blurb reads – 'How to create memorable voices and fictional conversations that crackle with wit, tension and nuance'. The 'rules' for writing good dialogue are as true for the novelist as the scriptwriter, and certainly most for the writer on radio. Chiarella guides you through the steps, from first and foremost *listening*, to finally writing.

The Best of Hancock Ray Galton and Alan Simpson (Robson Books, 1993)

A selection of scripts from one of the finest British TV sitcoms ever produced. Many of the classic episodes are included, such as 'Twelve Angry Men' ('Does 'Magna Carta' mean nothing to you? Did She die in vain . . . ?'), 'The Two Murderers', and the aforementioned 'Blood Donor'. All of Hancock's trademark pomposity and bluster is hilariously brought to life on the page thanks to Galton and Simpson's brilliant scripts. The book also contains photographs from the series and behind the scenes (including one of the writers looking very tall), as well as specially commissioned cartoons illustrating scenes from each episode.

Son of Soup Rob Grant and Doug Naylor (Penguin, 1996)

The second volume of selected scripts (in reverse order) from each of the seasons of Grant and Naylor's hilarious sci-fi sitcom *Red Dwarf*. An absolute must for fans of the series, but equally useful for budding writers, demonstrating as it does, the writers' use of unusual settings and sci-fi style jargon to comic effect. The book contains the full length versions of each script, including lines that were cut prior to recording, as well as those that were recorded but never broadcast.

The Royle Family – The Scripts: Series 1
Caroline Aherne, Craig Cash, Henry Normal (Granada Media, 1999)

Does what it says on the tin! All the scripts from the first series of Aherne, Cash and Normal's hugely popular sitcom. A masterclass in economy of dialogue and setting. (So, taking our cue from these superb scripts, we have nothing more to say!)

Blackadder – The Whole Damn Dynasty!
Richard Curtis, Ben Elton, Rowan Atkinson and John Lloyd (Penguin, 1999)

The complete scripts from all four series, plus additional material such as a history of the Blackadders, Baldrick's family tree, a list of Blackadder's finest insults, and lots more.

Frasier Jefferson Graham (Pocket Books, 1996)
Official companion book to the series, looking at the history of the show, episode guides for the first three series, characters', writers' and performers' profiles, classic quotes, and the script to the pilot episode 'The Good Son' by David Angell, Peter Casey and David Lee.

The Best of Frasier (Channel 4 Books, 1999)
A collection of 15 scripts from the first six series. Featuring the work of numerous writers, this is a superb collection of hilarious scripts that bear all the hallmarks of classic *Frasier*: sophisticated, literate dialogue; strong, clearly defined characters; and airtight plots. The beauty of the *Frasier* scripts is that they embrace all styles of humour: farce, romantic comedy, high comedy, broad comedy and even slapstick on occasion. All of these elements are amply displayed within this book.

The Very Best of Friends Penny Stallings and David Wild (Channel 4 Books, 2000)
To the best of our knowledge, there are no collections of published *Friends* scripts on the market, but this book is very useful as, aside from the usual series history and episode guides, it contains a complete first draft script of the 'Ross' wedding' episode, entitled 'The One You Were Never Supposed To See', including the writers' (Michael Borkow) and producers' handwritten notes for changes. Fascinating stuff.

The Glums Frank Muir and Denis Norden (Robson Books, 1979)
A collection of 13 scripts from the 1970s TV adaptation of the popular 1950s radio characters. These scripts provided a great deal of amusement and inspiration in our youth, and if for no other reason, are worth mentioning here. Outside of that, they also provide the reader with classic examples of 1950s comedy at its best, courtesy of Muir and Norden ('Mr. Glum, hang on a sec', 'Sorry, Eth, I haven't got time for secs!'), corny, saucy (but never rude) and just plain funny.

Rising Damp – A Celebration Richard Webber
(Boxtree, 2001)
A detailed history of the series, including a biography of writer Eric Chappell, and a section on his opinions of current sitcoms.

Radio Comedy 1938–1968 Andy Foster and Steve Furst
(Virgin, 1996)
Fascinating guide to all the major comedy series from radio's 'Golden Age', including many obscurities. Contains details of programmes such as *Hancock's Half Hour* and *A Life of Bliss*, as well as giving an insight to the comedic climate of the times.

Radio Times Guide to TV Comedy Mark Lewisohn
(BBC Worldwide, 1998)
In our opinion author Mark Lewisohn deserves a medal, a Knighthood, a Pulitzer Prize, a stiff drink and a good lie down after completing such a thorough, detailed, comprehensive and painstakingly researched book. It lists every (repeat 'every') series, one-off special and short programme of every nationality, ever broadcast on British television in the name of comedy, from 1936 up to the point of publication (of course). You name it, Mark Lewisohn's written about it, and although he is human, and as susceptible to fallibility as the rest of us, if he hasn't covered every last programme, then he's damn close! An absolutely amazing reference work. We doff our caps to you, Mr Lewisohn.

The Internet

Whether you are interested in the history or 'how to' of sitcoms, the Internet contains information on almost anything you want to know . . . and lots of stuff you didn't want to know! Try typing 'Sitcom' or 'Comedy Writing' into a good search engine like:

www.google.com or www.dogpile.com

The sites below will also take you to lots of comedy material:

www.comedywriting.com
www.writersweekly.com

and for a UK perspective there's myriad fan and practical orientated comedy sites accessible through:
www.bbc.co.uk

If you are interested in being a member of the studio audience at a recording, you can get information from the BBC website above, or alternatively, check the comedy listings page in *Time Out* magazine.

Organisations

Check out the website for the British Society of Comedy Writers at:
www.bscw.co.uk

or contact them at the following address:

The British Society of Comedy Writers (BSCW)
61 Parry Road
Ashmore Park
Wolverhampton
WV11 2PS

Index